St. Thomas Aquinas On The Two Commandments Of Charity And The Ten Commandments Of The Law, Tr. By Father Rawes

ST. THOMAS AQUINAS

ON THE COMMANDMENTS.

LONDON:

ROBSON AND SONS, PRINTERS, PANCRAS ROAD, N.W.

Little Books of the Holy Ghost.
No. I.

ST. THOMAS AQUINAS

ON

THE TWO COMMANDMENTS OF CHARITY

AND

THE TEN COMMANDMENTS OF THE LAW.

TRANSLATED, WITH PRAYERS ADDED, BY
FATHER RAWES, D.D.

'Let Thy tender mercies come unto me, and I shall live;
for Thy law is my meditation' (Ps. cxviii. 77).

LONDON: BURNS AND OATES.

TO THE

REV. FATHER RAWES, S.T.D.

MY DEAR FATHER,

I am glad to see that you have begun not only the greater series of books in the 'Library of the Holy Ghost,' but also a smaller and more popular series, in the 'Little Books of the Holy Ghost,' which will bring the devotion more readily within the reach of a larger number.

The greater series opens very fittingly with St. Thomas's treatise on the Blessed Sacrament, because it anticipates and answers a thought which might arise in some minds. St. Teresa had a singular devotion to the Holy Ghost; but she was jealously watchful against any doctrine which does not centre in the Incarnation, and derive all truth and grace from the Sacred Humanity. It is through the In-

carnate Son that we receive the Spirit of
adoption.   Jesus breathed upon the Apostles, and they received the Holy Ghost;
and we share, through them, in that mission of the Paraclete.   The first time we
read the Name of the Holy Ghost, as the
Third Person of the Ever-blessed Trinity,
is in the words of the Annunciation, ' The
Holy Ghost shall come upon thee.'   Therefore it is that devotion to the Holy Ghost
vivifies with a special light and grace our
adoration of the Sacred Humanity and of
the Blessed Sacrament, and our filial love
to the Mother of God.

You have also, I think, chosen well
St. Thomas's exposition of the Ten Commandments as the opening of the lesser
series of ' Little Books of the Holy Ghost.'
It is a work which ought to be in the
hands of the faithful, and on the lips of
our priests.

One such solid book of the ages of faith
outweighs many manuals, however pious,
of our softer days.

In thus putting the two series of books and the devotion under the patronage of St. Thomas, whom our Holy Father has so lately set before us as our teacher, you have given to them a solid foundation in the dogmatic theology of the Church.

As to 'The Holy Ghost, the Sanctifier,' I will not fail to use what free time I can to get it ready. Meanwhile I will only say that it seems strange that any one should have thought the devotion to the Holy Ghost to be either novel or unusual in the Catholic Church. As St. Augustin says of miracles, that by their multitude they pass unperceived, so with the devotion to the Holy Ghost.

The Catholic Church has no distinct festival for the First Person of the Ever-blessed Trinity: but for the Second and for the Third Persons of the Holy Trinity the Church has sanctioned and always used distinct and proper devotions.

As to the Eternal Son, a whole series of festivals from Christmas to the Ascension

sets Him before us in His Advent, His
Incarnation, His Life, His Redemption, and
His return to the glory of the Father.

As to the Holy Ghost, the Feast of Pentecost sets before us His Advent; and a
whole series of acts of distinct and special
adoration brings before us His abiding
Presence ; His perpetual Assistance in the
Church, as its Guide ; and His indwelling
in every faithful soul, as our Sanctifier;
for instance, the *Votive Mass of the Holy
Ghost ;* the solemn invocation in the Holy
Mass, *Veni, Sanctificator, Omnipotens,
Æterne Deus ;* the *Veni Creator Spiritus,*
in the ordination of Priests, in the opening of Œcumenical Councils, and Provin-
cial and Diocesan Synods; add to this
the whole office for Confirmation : moreover, the *Veni Creator Spiritus ;* the *Veni
Sancte Spiritus ;* the *Adsumus Domine
Sancte Spiritus,* which are prayers of the
Pontificale and the *Rituale* of the Catholic Church.   To these it is hardly needful
to add the many indulgenced prayers and

devotions in authorised manuals; the *Office of the Holy Ghost;* the *Litany;* the *Novena* used in Rome; and I know not what besides.   If the devotion to the Holy Ghost be to any one novel or unusual, a moment's thought will transfer this reflection from the Catholic worship to his own daily prayers.

Every day I pray that the consciousness of our great vocation to be Disciples and Servants of the Holy Ghost, by our regeneration, may be deepened in us all, and diffused throughout the Christian world.

Believe me always, my dear Father,

Yours affectionately in Jesus Christ,

HENRY EDWARD,
Cardinal Archbishop of Westminster.

Archbishop's House,
Oct. 22, 1879.

JOHN JOSEPH KEANE,

BY THE GRACE OF GOD AND

THE FAVOUR OF THE APOSTOLIC SEE,

BISHOP OF RICHMOND,.

TO THE FAITHFUL OF THE DIOCESE, GRACE

AND PEACE IN OUR LORD.

Beloved Brethren, — Having requested all the Pastors throughout the Diocese to establish in their various Missions the Confraternity of the Servants of the Holy Ghost, and desiring that you should heartily respond to the holy invitation thus extended to you, we deem it our duty to make known to you in this manner the nature of this devotion, and our reasons for desiring that it should be embraced by all the faithful of the Diocese.

Devotion to the Holy Ghost is a most natural offspring of Christian faith, because the Holy Ghost is the very life and soul of the Christian dispensation.

The Holy Ghost is the Infinite Love of God, proceeding from the Father and the Son, and perfecting the Being of the adorable Trinity, according to that sublime utterance of St. John, 'Deus charitas est,' 'God is Love.'

It was through love that God created and redeemed us; therefore it is that the Holy Scripture shows us that the works of creation and redemption, wrought by the power of the Father and the wisdom of the Son, are finished and perfected by the action of the Spirit of Love, the Holy Ghost. Hence, when our Divine Redeemer had completed His work on earth, and was about to return to His Father, He said to His disciples : ' It is expedient for you that I go ; for if I go not, the Paraclete will not come to you ; but if I go, I will send Him to you' (John xvi. 7). According to our Saviour's promise, the Holy Ghost came on Whitsunday, from the bosom of the Father and the Son, to finish and carry on for ever the work of Their mercy. He became the soul of the Christian Church, making it into a living body; and all its life has ever since come from Him and depended on Him, and so shall continue till the end of the world. All the divine truth that has ever been taught by the Church, or has ever illumined the minds of her children, has come from the Holy Ghost, 'the Spirit of Truth.' All the grace that has ever been dispensed in her Sacraments, or has ever wrought the sanctification of souls, is the work of the Holy Ghost, 'the Giver of Life.' Whenever we ask a spiritual favour from Almighty God, through the merits of our Divine Saviour, or through the intercession of the Blessed Virgin and the Saints, whether we think of the Holy Ghost or not, the blessing given is the outpouring of His love, the grace received is His gift. Whenever we strive to advance in the way to heaven, to climb the ladder of holiness, the power by which we advance is the action of the Holy Ghost. Whenever we think a good thought,

say a good word, or do a good action, it is
by and through 'the Spirit of God dwelling
in us' that we do it, since St. Paul teaches
us that we cannot even utter the holy Name
of Jesus 'but by the Holy Ghost' (1 Cor.
xii. 3).

How great, therefore, and how constant
is our debt of gratitude to the Holy Ghost!
How intimately is our whole spiritual life
pervaded by His influence! The more we
learn of our interior life the more we must
learn of the work wrought by the power
and the love of the Holy Ghost. Not to
think of this would surely indicate strange
thoughtlessness about spiritual things; and
to think of it, and not turn constantly
toward the Holy Ghost in thanksgiving, as
well as in supplication, would surely be
the height of ingratitude. Yet, alas, how
much of such thoughtlessness and such ingratitude has not the Holy Spirit to endure
at our hands!

In this age, when the spirit of error is
trying to make men believe that their life

is only like that of the beasts of the field, the Church, guided ever by the hand of God, turns the attention of her children, perhaps more specially than at any previous time, to the interior and supernatural life of their souls, of which the Holy Ghost is the Author.   The devotion to the Holy Ghost, together with the teaching concerning our spiritual life with which that devotion is inseparably connected, is unquestionably the best antidote for the materialistic and degrading tendencies of our times.

This general and providential tendency toward devotion to the Holy Ghost has taken form in the Confraternity of the Servants of the Holy Ghost, established in London under the patronage of Cardinal Manning.   It had the warm approval of Pope Pius IX., and our Holy Father Leo XIII.* approved it in March 1878, and, on the 6th of April 1879, raised it to the

* On March 10, 1878, Leo XIII. erected the Confraternity and gave it many Indulgences.

dignity of an Archconfraternity, with power to aggregate Confraternities throughout the world. A devotion so conformable to the present providential tendency of the Church, and which has received so solemn approval from two successive Sovereign Pontiffs, cannot fail to recommend itself strongly to all Christians. And especially do we desire to foster this devotion in the Diocese of Richmond, since, from the moment that Almighty God was pleased to lay the burden of its spiritual care on our weak shoulders, we felt impelled to look to the Holy Ghost as the source of all the wisdom and strength needful for the worthy discharge of so weighty a duty, and to put all our administration under His special protection. It is therefore our earnest desire that a Confraternity of the Servants of the Holy Ghost should be established in every Mission throughout the Diocese, and that every Catholic that has made his or her First Communion should be enrolled in this beautiful devotion.

No one need be withheld by the fear of multiplying devotions, or of undertaking too many pious practices. It is, indeed, far from advisable to have too many devotions; but the spirit of piety cannot but impel us to have *some;*—we should choose the best, and no one certainly can fail to recognise that this devotion to the Holy Ghost must be among the very best. It is equally unadvisable to undertake too many pious practices; for experience shows that the effort to say too many prayers and crowd too many exercises into the time that can be daily given to them is ordinarily the destruction of attention and fervour in all the prayers that are said. But the devotion to the Holy Ghost is not liable to this objection. As it is clearly stated on the certificate of membership, the only obligation is *to be enrolled,*— with a sincere desire and resolution to love and honour the Holy Ghost, to think of Him more frequently and fervently, and to correspond to His grace more faithfully.

It is indeed *advisable* that such devotion to the Holy Ghost should manifest itself in some daily practices, such as saying seven times the *Glory be to the Father* to ask the seven Gifts of the Holy Ghost, or the recitation of the *Veni Sancte Spiritus*, or the *Veni Creator Spiritus*, or the saying of the *Little Office of the Holy Ghost*, or some portion of it. But none of these practices are of obligation, and therefore they need not inspire dread or scruple.

It is recommended that the members should assemble for public exercises once a month. This, again, is not obligatory; but it is very useful, and our Holy Father has granted an indulgence of 100 days to the members who will attend the monthly meetings. In order that these meetings may be more systematic and profitable, it is our intention to propose, ere long, a form of Sodality organisation for the members, and a *Little Office of the Holy Ghost* which might very usefully be recited at the meetings, or as an act of private devotion.

We therefore most earnestly invite all Catholics who have received their First Communion to respond to this our recommendation, when made known to them by their Pastors, and to give in their names without delay for enrolment. A certificate of membership will be given to each one, which also contains a brief summary of the indulgences to be gained by the Servants of the Holy Ghost and the acts of devotion recommended to them. To these is added a short prayer to the Holy Ghost for the enlightenment and conversion of all the souls in the Diocese of Richmond that are outside of the one fold, which we request all the members to say every day, as an act of fraternal charity toward their poor separated brethren.

May our heart be gladdened by a ready and devout response to this invitation on the part of all our faithful people; and may this devotion draw down incalculable blessings on the Diocese, and give endless glory to the Father, the Son, and the Holy Ghost!

Given at Richmond this 18th day of October, the Festival of St. Luke the Evangelist, in the year of our Lord 1879.

✠ JOHN JOSEPH KEANE,
Bishop of Richmond.

PREFACE.

———

MEN break the commandments of God very fearfully in these days, as they have broken them in all days. The reason is that they do not think of them, and do not try to understand the greatness of their beauty.

We all of us fail much in this matter. If we thought of these holy commandments more, meditating oftener on the law of God, we should keep them far better than we do. We should try to enter into their depths of light, seeing in them more clearly the finger of God, and hearing His voice in them more plainly; the voice that was heard among the thunders of Horeb, and the light that was seen amid the lightning-flashes when 'all Mount Sinai was on a smoke because the Lord was come down

on it in fire, and the smoke rose from it as
out of a furnace, and all the mount was
terrible' (Ex. xix. 18).

Because I have a very great desire that
all the Servants of the Holy Ghost may
always keep the ten commandments shrined
in the faithfulness of their hearts, I have
translated this little treatise of the Angelic
Doctor. No one teaches as he does. His
soul was always full of love and full of
light. Read what our Holy Father Leo
XIII. says about him in his last splendid
Encyclical. His words there have crowned
St. Thomas with a very bright crown. He
has shown how no one can be compared
with him for defending and instructing
the Church. It is not likely, he tells us,
that there will be any mightier intellect
than his, nor that reason will ever give
greater help to the faith than was given
by him.

You, the Servants of the Holy Ghost,
ought to rejoice greatly in that Encyclical
of our Holy Father. The first volume of

'The Library of the Holy Ghost' is *St. Thomas Aquinas on the Adorable Sacrament of the Altar*. The second volume will be *St. Thomas Aquinas on the Holy Ghost*. Because of this, I cannot but feel that the words of the Vicar of Christ are laden with blessing for our Library and our work, giving them sanction also and approval, at any rate implicitly, because we desire to learn from this greatest of teachers, who, as Leo XIII. says, is 'likened to the sun, for he warmed the whole earth with the fire of his holiness, and filled the whole earth with the splendour of his teaching.'

In the second volume of the Library, which will soon be in your hands if God bless the undertaking, there is a preface about St. Thomas in his greatness and his brightness, and the majestic grandeur of his work. That preface was written some months ago, when I never dreamed of a blessing so great as this Encyclical of our Holy Father, Leo XIII. ; and now it seems to me to have, in a special way, the approbation of the Vicar of Jesus Christ.

Again, this series of 'Little Books of the Holy Ghost' begins with the Angelic Doctor's words. This first book is *St. Thomas Aquinas on the Ten Commandments*. I chose that book, first, because of the unspeakable worth of the law of God; and, next, because we are taught in it by one who was truly a cherubic saint, a soul filled with the light of heavenly wisdom. His words, more than all other words, set forth the grandeur of the commandments of God.

Another quotation about him I should like to make from the Encyclical. It is a passage from a sermon of Innocent VI.: 'His doctrine, above all other doctrines, with the one exception of the Holy Scriptures, has such a propriety of words, such a method of explanation, such a truth of opinions, that no one who holds it will ever be found to have strayed from the path of truth; whereas any one who has attacked it has always been suspected as to the truth.'

For us St. Thomas leads the way, in the luminous might of his words, and heads the work that we have begun in our Library. That work is under the protection of the Blessed Spirit of God. It is for His glory and for the salvation of souls. Many, I think, will see the finger of God, when they read this Encyclical of the Vicar of our Lord. It is he who founded the Confraternity, and then the Archconfraternity of the Servants of the Holy Ghost. With all my heart I thank God for this letter of Leo XIII.

At the risk of seeming to say too much about myself, I will venture to mention two things. First, I was received into the One Church of God on St. Thomas's Feast. Thanks to this Angelic Saint and to the Beloved Disciple from whom he drank the depths of his knowledge, I have had from that day to this day an ever-deepening certainty that the Roman Church is 'of God, and the whole world is seated in wickedness' (1 John v. 19). Next, two years and a half ago, I gave the first retreat in honour of the Holy Ghost, in the Church of St. Mary of the Angels, Bayswater. Some Servants of the Holy Ghost put up a stained-glass window in remembrance of the retreat, and in thanksgiving for many spiritual blessings received in those days. The subject of the window is the Saint from whom in that Pentecost week we learned about the Adorable Paraclete and the mysteries of the kingdom of God—St. Thomas Aquinas, the Angel of the schools.

St. Thomas's *Treatise on the Commandments* is plain, short, practical, and full of instruction. There is a simplicity of strength about it which is to me very attractive. You will see for yourselves how wonderfully the Saint illustrates each point from the Scriptures of God. As with all his writings, so here, the manner is worthy of the words; and the words, so far as man's words can be, are worthy of the truths which they enshrine and unfold.

It seems to me that the book might be used so as to be very useful for meditations; and therefore I have marked the points in Clarendon and Italics, as I have already done in *The Bread of Life.*

I have added a prayer at the end of each chapter, because the way of the commandments is the way of everlasting life; and we can only go along the road of life by grace; and they who pray find the grace that they need. The prayerless soul is ever hanging over the bottomless pit; but the praying soul lives with Saints and Angels and the Mother of God in the light of that kingdom which needs no light of the sun or moon to lighten it, because the glory of the Holy Ghost enlightens it, and the Heart of Jesus is its lamp.

I have also added two thanksgivings, one at the beginning, and one at the end, because we do not thank God half enough for His miracles and Saints of the law of nature and the law of Moses, nor for His Ten Commandments.

Servants of the Holy Ghost, I wish very much to help you in the way of life by these words of St. Thomas on keeping the commandments of God. As St. Paul tells us, speaking of Jesus (Eph. ii. 18), 'By Him we have access in one Spirit to the Father.' I ask you to pray for me that I may 'find mercy of the Lord in that day' (2 Tim. i. 18). Pray that we all of us may be found watching and waiting in the day of our Master's coming.

Feast of the Stigmata of
St. Francis of Assisi, 1879.

CONTENTS.

CONTENTS.

𝔖t. 𝔗𝔥𝔬𝔪𝔞𝔰 𝔄𝔮𝔲𝔦𝔫𝔞𝔰, 𝔄𝔫𝔤𝔢𝔩𝔦𝔠 𝔇𝔬𝔠𝔱𝔬𝔯,

PRAY FOR US WHO LOVE TO LEARN ABOUT THE
LAW OF GOD FROM THEE.

CHAPTER I.

OF THE LAW OF NATURE AND THE LAW OF
SCRIPTURE ; AND ALSO OF THE DIFFERENCE
BETWEEN THE LAW OF MOSES AND THE
LAW OF CHRIST.

THREE things are necessary to man for salvation, that is to say, 1. a knowledge of what he must believe ; 2. a knowledge of what he must desire ; 3. a knowledge of what he must do. The first is taught in the Creed, where there is handed down a knowledge of the articles of faith ; the second is taught in the Lord's Prayer ; the third is taught in the law.

I. Our purpose now is to speak of the things that we must do ; and for the treat-

B

ment of this question we find that there is a
fourfold law.

1. **The law of nature.** That is nothing
else than the light of understanding implanted in us by God, by which we know
what to do and what to avoid. God gave
man this light and this law in creation.
Yet many think that ignorance excuses
them from keeping this law. Against
them the Prophet says (Ps. iv. 6), ' Many
say, Who showeth us good things ?' They
speak thus, as if they did not know what
to do. But he answers them in the same
place (ver. 7), 'The light of Thy countenance, O Lord, is signed upon us.' This
is the light of the understanding by which
we know what to do. No one, for instance,
is ignorant that he ought not to do to
others what he is unwilling to have done
to himself. Other like things are known
in the same way.

2. **The law of concupiscence.** God
having given man the law of nature in his
creation, the devil planted in him another

law, that is, the law of concupiscence. So long as the soul of the first man was subject to God by keeping His commands, his flesh was in all things subject to his soul or reason. But, when the devil by his wiles drew man away from keeping God's commandments, then his flesh rebelled against his reason. Thus, then, it comes about that man, in his reason wishing what is good, yet by concupiscence inclines to what is evil. St. Paul says (Rom. vii. 23), ' I see another law in my members fighting against the law of my mind.' Hence it often happens that the law of concupiscence corrupts the law of nature and the right order of reason. Therefore the Apostle adds, ' Bringing me into captivity to the law of sin that is in my members.'

The law of Scripture. When the law of nature was corrupted by the law of concupiscence, it became necessary that man should first be brought back again from sin ; and then be led on to works of holi-

ness. For this was needed the law of
Scripture.* But man is drawn from evil
and led to good by two motives, that is,
a. by fear, and, *b.* by love.

3. *a.* **Fear : the law of Moses.** As a
rule, the first reason why any one begins to
avoid sin is the thought of the last judgment and hell. Therefore Scripture says
(Ecclus. i. 16), ' The fear of the Lord is the
beginning of wisdom ;' and again (ver. 27),
' The fear of the Lord driveth out sin.'
Though one who keeps from sin through
fear† is not just, yet his justification is
beginning. In this way man was kept
from evil and led to good by the law of
Moses. When he made that law void he
was punished with death ; as the Apostle
says (Heb. x. 28), ' A man making void
the law of Moses dieth without any mercy
under two or three witnesses.'

* The law of Moses is called the law of Scripture. Thus, Hugh of St. Victor has a treatise,
' On the Sacraments of the Law of Nature and of
the Written Law.'

† That   fear ' simply servile.'

4. *b.* **Love: the law of Christ.** The law of Moses, drawing men from evil by. fear, was not enough. It held the hand, but did not hold the heart. Another way therefore was needed to keep men from evil and lead them to good, that is, the way of love. Thus, then, was given the law of love, the evangelical law, the law of Christ.

II. Bear in mind that there is a three-fold difference between the law of fear and the law of love.

1. **Slaves and freemen.** The law of fear makes us slaves, while the law of love makes us free. He who acts only from fear acts like a slave; but he who acts from love acts as a free man. St. Paul says (2 Cor. iii. 17), 'Where the Spirit of the Lord is, there is liberty.' Such men, like sons, act from love.

2. **Temporal and everlasting rewards.** The keepers of the first law were promised temporal goods. Isaias says (i. 19), 'If you be willing, and will hearken to Me,

you shall eat the good things of the land.'
But the keepers of the second law are promised heavenly rewards. Jesus says (St.
Matt. xix. 17), 'If thou wilt enter into
life, keep the commandments.' The Holy
Baptist says (St. Matt. iii. 2), 'Do penance,
for the kingdom of Heaven is at hand.'

3. **Heavy and light.** The first law, the
law of Moses, was heavy; but the second
law, the law of Christ, is light. Of the
law of Moses, St. Peter said to the Pharisees, who were contending for its observ-
ance (Acts xv. 10), 'Why tempt you God
to put a yoke upon the necks of the disciples which neither our fathers nor we
have been able to bear?' Of His own law,
Jesus Himself said (St. Matt. xi. 30), 'My
yoke is sweet, and My burden light.' The
Apostle also says (Rom. viii. 15), 'You
have not received the spirit of bondage
again in fear; but you have received the
Spirit of adoption of sons, whereby we cry,
Abba, Father.'

*Thanksgiving for the miracles and Saints of
the law of nature, and for the miracles
and Saints of the law of Moses.*

O adorable Trinity, Three Persons and
One God, Thou uncreated Source of life, I
am Thy creature, and Thou hast made me
for Thyself. O God, Father, Son, and
Holy Ghost, Thou art the one principle of
creatures, their one Maker and their one
Lord. Having made us, Thou hast given
us Thy law to keep. It is a law, holy and
beautiful and divine; an image of Thy
goodness, and a shadow of Thy light. According to the manner of Thy gift it has
been a threefold law, always good, like
Thyself. Coming from Thy love and wisdom, it has been always fitted for the
time.

I adore Thee, my God, in the law of
nature and the dawn of Thy revelation of
love. I bless and thank Thee for the
mighty Saints whom Thou didst raise up in
that law. Great were the miracles that

Thou didst show them, and overflowing were Thy revelations and inspirations of grace.

'Seeing that the wickedness of men was great on the earth, and that all the thought of their heart was bent upon evil at all time,' Thou didst 'rain upon the earth forty days and forty nights,' and didst destroy man, whom Thou hadst created, 'from the face of the earth.'

When 'the earth was of one tongue and the same speech,' and when men were building on the 'plain in the land of Sennaar' 'a city and a tower, the top whereof' might 'reach to Heaven,' Thou didst 'there confound their tongue,' and they could not any longer 'understand one another's speech.' Then Thine arm 'scattered them from that place into all lands.'

The cities of the plain, in the hideousness of their corruption, being hateful to Thee, were swept away by the 'brimstone and fire' which Thou didst rain upon them. When Thy servant Abraham 'looked towards Sodom and Gomorrha, and the whole land of that country,' ' early in the morning,' ' he saw the ashes rise up from the earth as the smoke of a furnace.'

When Lot and his wife and two daughters were flying to Segor, ' his wife, looking behind her, was turned into a statue of salt' by Thee.

I adore Thee, O ever-blessed Trinity, in these miracles of Thy avenging wrath.

I praise Thee for our first father and mother, Adam and Eve, in their penance and sorrow for sin.

I praise Thee for Abel, Priest, and Virgin-Martyr, and Shepherd; and for the blood that speaketh better things than his.

I praise Thee for Henoch, who ' walked with God, and was seen no more, for God took him.' I praise Thee for his hidden resting-place, in which Thou dost keep him with Elias, that in the days of antichrist they may be the two witnesses clothed in sackcloth and slain for the Son of man.

I praise Thee for saving Thy servant
Noe, with his family, in the ark, from the
destroying flood. He 'found grace before'
Thee. He 'was a just and perfect man;'
and he 'walked with' Thee in the evil
days.

I praise Thee for faithful Abraham, Thy
friend.

I praise Thee for Isaac, his son of promise, lying as a willing sacrifice on the
altar of 'the pile of wood.' Thou didst
save him by the voice of Thy angel, twice
calling to his father from Heaven.

I praise Thee for the sufferings and vic-
tories of Jacob, and for the change of his
name to Israel.

I praise Thee for Joseph, the giver of
bread, in Egypt.

I praise Thee for 'Melchisedech, the
king of Salem, bringing forth bread and
wine.' He was Thy priest, 'for he was
the priest of the most high God.'

I praise Thee for the patience of Job,
of whom Thy word says, 'that man was

simple and upright, and fearing God and avoiding evil.'

I praise Thee for Thy gifts of grace to Sara and Rebecca and Rachel.

I adore Thee, my God, in the law of Moses, Thy servant, and in the morning of Thy revelation of love. I bless and thank Thee for the mighty Saints whom Thou didst raise up in that law. Great were the miracles that Thou didst show them, and overflowing were Thy revelations and inspirations of grace.

In ten plagues Thou didst lay Thy hand heavily on idolatrous Egypt. Thy angel slew the first-born : Thou didst cover the land with darkness for three days; Thou didst turn the Nile into a river of blood.

By the lifting of the rod of Moses, Thou didst divide the Red Sea, and Israel went 'through the midst of the sea on dry ground,' when ' the water was as a wall on their right hand and their left.' Thou didst save Thy people from the enemy ; 'and as the Egyptians were fleeing away, the waters came upon them,' and Thou didst 'shut them up in the middle of the waves.'

As Thy people went through the desert, Thou didst go 'before them to show them the way by day in a pillar of a cloud, and by night in a pillar of fire; that' Thou mightest 'be the guide of their journey at both times.' So great was Thy goodness that 'there never failed the pillar of the cloud by day nor the pillar of fire by night before the people.' For forty years Thou didst feed them with manna, and for forty years Thou didst keep their clothes from wearing out. In Thy word it is said, 'He hath brought you forty years through the desert: your garments are not worn out, neither are the shoes of your feet consumed with age. You have not eaten bread, nor have you drunk wine or strong drink, that you may know that I am the Lord.'

Before Thy people set out on their desert journey Thou didst give them Thy Ten Commandments on Horeb, when Moses went up into the mountain in the midst of the cloud, and was with Thee forty days and forty nights. Then the sight of Thy glory on the top of the mount was like a burning fire.

. Thou didst bring Thy people into the promised land through the parted waters of Jordan rushing swiftly in flood. Thou didst cast down the walls of Jericho at the sound of the trumpets of Israel. Josue, guided by Thee, said to the sun and moon, ' Move not, O sun, toward Gabaon, nor thou, O moon, toward the valley of Ajalon.' By Thy almighty hand ' the sun stood still in the midst of heaven, and hasted not to go down the space of one day.' In Thy word it is written, ' There was not before nor after so long a day, the Lord obeying the voice of a man and fighting for Israel.'

In the feast of Baltassar, amid the praise of gods of gold and silver, and brass and iron, and wood and stone, in the hour of doom, the fingers of a man's hand wrote on the surface of the wall; ' and the king beheld the joints of the hand that wrote.'

At Thy command an ass spoke with the voice of a man to reprove the madness of a wicked prophet.

Jonas was 'three days and three nights' in the 'great fish' that had been prepared by Thee. To Thee he prayed from the 'deep in the heart of the sea,' where Thy floods compassed him and Thy waves passed over him. At Thy word he stood 'upon the dry land.'

With pitch and hair and fat Daniel destroyed the great dragon which the Babylonians worshipped. Twice didst Thou bring him safely from the den of lions.

By Thee the Three Children came unharmed from the burning fiery furnace.

Guided by Thy Angel Raphael, Tobias drove away the unclean devil, and healed the blindness of his father.

By faith Thy servants 'conquered kingdoms, wrought justice, obtained promises, stopped the mouths of lions, quenched the violence of fire, escaped the edge of the sword, recovered strength from weakness, became valiant in battle, put to flight the armies of the aliens. Women received their dead raised to life again.'

I adore Thee, O ever-blessed Trinity, in these miracles of Thy anger and Thy love.

O my God, I praise Thee for Moses Thy great lawgiver, and for Josue, the virgin-warrior of Israel.

I praise Thee for Gedeon and Barac and Jephte and Samson and Samuel.

I praise Thee for David the shepherd-king of Israel, the man after Thine 'own heart; for Ezechias, who 'did that which was pleasing' in Thy sight; and for Josias, who walked in Thy ways, and 'declined not, either to the right hand or the left.'

I praise Thee for Elias, who 'was magnified in his wondrous works,' and who was 'taken up in a whirlwind of fire, in a chariot of fiery horses.' He is waiting with Henoch in their hidden resting-place, upheld by Thee, till the time of their witness against antichrist in the days of terror that must be shortened for the sake of the elect.

In Thy word it is written, ' Henoch pleased
God, and was translated into Paradise, that
he may give repentance to the nations.'
Of Elias it is written, he is ' registered in
the judgments of times to appease the
wrath of the Lord, to reconcile the heart of
the father to the son, and to restore the
tribes of Jacob.'

I praise Thee for Eliseus, who was filled
with the spirit of Elias, and whose ' body
prophesied after death.' ' In his life he
did great wonders, and in death he wrought
miracles.'

I praise Thee for Nehemias, who ' wept
and mourned for many days, and fasted
and prayed before' Thee, because ' the wall
of Jerusalem was broken down and the
gates thereof burnt with fire ;' and for
Esdras, who ' had prepared his heart to
seek the law of the Lord, and to do and to
teach in Israel the commandments and
judgment.'

I praise Thee for the splendour of Thy
four prophets, like the four living creatures

before Thy throne; for Isaias and Jeremias and Ezechiel and Daniel.

I praise Thee for Baruch, who said, 'This is the book of the commandments of God, and the law that is for ever. All they that keep it shall come to life; but they that have forsaken it, to death. Return, O Jacob, and take hold of it; walk in the way by its brightness, in the presence of the light thereof.'

I praise Thee for the majesty of Osee and Joel and Amos and Abdias and Jonas and Micheas and Habacuc and Nahum and Sophonias and Aggeus and Zacharias and Malachias.

I praise Thee for Ruth, who came to 'Bethlehem in the beginning of the barley harvest,' and who 'gleaned the ears of corn after the reapers;' for Debbora, the prophetess who 'sat under a palm-tree,' and 'judged the people;' and for Anna, who prayed to Thee 'shedding many tears,' with 'her heart full of grief,' and who gave Samuel her son to minister before Thy face.

Israel.' ' The Holy Ghost was in him, and he had received an answer from the Holy Ghost that he should not see death before he had seen the Christ of the Lord ; and he came by the Spirit into the temple.' Then he took Jesus into his arms, and blessed Mary and Joseph.

I praise Thee for the Holy Baptist, the messenger of the covenant, and the baptiser of the Word Incarnate.

I praise Thee for holy Joseph, the spouse of the Mother of God, and the foster-father of Jesus.

Glorious art Thou, my God, in all Thy signs and wonders from the beginning of the world ; and glorious art Thou in the Saints, who waited for the coming of the Messias ! They loved Thee and kept Thy law through the four thousand years of His tarrying. In Thy Spirit all holy men and women were longing for Him ; and to Him were ever turning the hearts of patri- archs and kings, of seers and prophets of Israel.

O adorable Trinity, how glorious Thou art in the light of love that blessed the world through the days before the flood; and how glorious Thou art from Thy covenant with Noe to Thy covenant with the father of the faithful!

O adorable Trinity, how glorious Thou art in the light shining from Abraham to Moses; and in the light that ever fell on the tabernacle and the temple and the innermost shrine!

O adorable Trinity, types and signs and prophecies and sacrifices of Jesus were aflame with Thy light. In them shone the brightness of Thy wisdom. The odour of sweetness ceased not in Thy temple; and its venerable courts were worn by the footsteps of Thy Saints. They longed for 'the desire of the everlasting hills,' and waited for Him lovingly as He tarried and did not come!

O Father, Son, and Holy Ghost, one Lord, one God, I bless and praise Thee for Thy love and wisdom in the ancient

years. I adore Thee in all preludes of the
Dayspring, and in all heralds of the Word
made flesh. I adore Thee in the light
that fell on the earthly paradise, and in
the greater light that shone from Simeon's
arms when 'the Desired of all nations'
came to His temple suddenly!

CHAPTER II.

OF THE EFFECTS OF THE LAW OF CHARITY.

THERE is, then, as has been said, a fourfold law. The first is, the law of nature
which God implanted in man at his creation. The second is the law of concupiscence. The third is the law of Scripture.
The fourth is the law of charity and grace,
that is, the law of Christ.

But it is evident that all men cannot
toil in getting knowledge; and therefore
Jesus gave us a law, so short that it may
be known by all, and so plain, that no one

can be excused by ignorance from keeping
it.   This is the law of the love of God; as
St. Paul says (Rom. ix. 28), 'A short word
shall the Lord make upon the earth.'

I. Now we ought to understand that
this law should be the rule of all human
acts.   In things made, a work is said to be
good and right when it is according to
rule.   So a work of man is right and virtuous when it agrees with the law of the
love of God.   Such a work cannot be right
or good or perfect when it is out of harmony
with God's law; but being in harmony
with that rule it is good.

Further, we ought to know that this law
of the love of God works in man four
things that are to be sought for most earnestly.

1. **Spiritual life.** Naturally the loved
one is found in the heart of the lover, and
therefore the lover of God has God in himself; as St. John says (1 Ep. iv. 16), ' He
that abideth in charity abideth in God,
and God in him.'   It is the nature of love

also to transform the lover into the thing loved. Hence, if we love things worthless and perishing we become worthless and weak ourselves : as Osee says (ix. 10), 'They became abominable as those things were which they loved.' If, on the other hand, we love God we are made divine ; for St. Paul teaches that (1 Cor. vi. 17), ' He who is joined to the Lord is one spirit.' St. Augustin says, 'As the soul is the life of the body, so God is the life of the soul.' This is easily seen. We say that the body lives by the soul when it has proper vital functions, and works and is moved. When, however, the soul leaves the body, then the body neither works nor is moved. So the soul works with holiness and perfection when it works by charity, for by charity God dwells in it; but without charity it does not work; for in St. John's words (1 Ep. iii. 14), ' He that loveth not abideth in death.'

We must carefully bear in mind that if any one have all gifts of the Holy Ghost, which can exist without charity, he has not life. Thus he may have the gift of tongues or the gift of faith, or other like gifts; but these things without charity do not give life. You may wrap up a dead body in gold and precious stones; but dead that body remains. You see, then, the first effect of charity.

2. **Faithfulness.** By charity we keep the commandments of God. St. Gregory says, 'The love of God is never idle. Where that love is it does great things; and that which works not is thus known not to be love.' A sure sign, therefore, of charity is promptness in fulfilling God's commands. We have seen great and difficult things done for the sake of one who is loved; and our Lord says (St. John xiv. 23), 'If any one love Me he will keep My word.'

Here we should observe that the whole law is fulfilled by him who keeps the law and the commandment of the love of God. Now God's commandments are of two kinds. Some are affirmative; and these are kept by charity, because the fulness of the law which consists in the commandments is the love by which the commandments are kept. Others are prohibitory; and these also are kept by charity, because, as St. Paul says (1 Cor. xiii. 4), charity ‘ dealeth not perversely.’

3. **Confidence in God.** Charity is our safeguard in all trials. If a man have charity, no evils hurt him, but all are turned to his good. It is said (Rom. viii. 28), ‘ We know that to them who love God all things work together unto good.’ Nay more; things hard and difficult seem easy and pleasant to one who loves, as we can easily see for ourselves.

4. **Everlasting life.** Charity leads us to everlasting life. The beatitude of heaven is promised only to those who have charity; for all things are not enough for this blessedness without love. St. Paul says (2 Tim. iv. 8), ‘ As to the rest, there is laid up for me a crown of justice, which the Lord, the just Judge, will give to me in

that day ; and not only to me, but to them also who love His coming.'

Besides, difference in beatitude is given for difference in charity, and not for difference in any other virtue. There have been many who have fasted more than the Apostles, but the Apostles surpass all others in beatitude because of the greatness of their love. For, as St. Paul says (Rom. viii. 23), the Apostles had 'the first-fruits of the Spirit.' Hence difference in beatitude is from difference in love; and thus are seen four of the works that charity does in us.

II. We must not, however, pass by six other effects of charity in the soul.

1. **Forgiveness.** Charity works forgiveness of sin. This we can see from what happens among men. If any one offend another and afterwards come to be much loved by him, then, because of love, the offender is forgiven. So God also forgives the sins of those who love Him. 'Charity covereth a multitude of sins' (1 Pet. iv. 8).

Well does St. Peter use the word 'covers,' for they are not seen by God so as to bring punishment. But Solomon (Prov. x. 12) says more; 'Charity covereth all sins.' This is seen best in St. Mary Magdalen. Our Lord said (St. Luke vii. 47), 'Many sins are forgiven her.' He also added the reason, 'because she hath loved much.'

It may be that some one will say, Then charity is enough for taking away sins, and repentance is not needed. Such a one should consider that no one loves truly who does not repent truly. For it is plain that the more we love any one, the more we must grieve if we offend him. This, then, is one effect of charity.

2. **Light.** Charity gives enlightenment of heart; when, as Job says (xxxvii. 19), 'We are wrapped up in darkness.' We often do not know what we ought to do or what we ought to seek for; and then love teaches us all things necessary to salvation: according to St. John's words (1 Ep. ii. 27), 'His unction teacheth you

of all things, and is truth.' This is so, because where charity is there is the Holy Ghost, who knows all things and leads us in the right way. Therefore it is said (Ecclus. ii. 10), 'Ye that fear the Lord love Him, and your hearts shall be enlightened.' They shall be enlightened to know all things needed for salvation.

3. **Joy**. Charity makes man perfect in joy. No one can have true joy if he have not love. If a man long greatly for anything he is without joy, without gladness, without rest, till he gain it. Now in temporal things we seek for that which we have not, while that which we have is little cared for, and sometimes even causes weariness in us. But in spiritual things it is otherwise. He who loves God has God; and thus a soul that loves and longs has rest in Him. St. John says (1 Ep. iv. 16), ' He that abideth in charity abideth in God, and God in him.'

4. **Peace**. Charity gives us perfect peace. It often happens, in things of this world,

that the attainment of an object greatly
desired brings no rest to the soul of the
seeker. So soon as one thing is gained he
begins to seek for something else. Isaias
says (lvii. 20, 21), 'The wicked are like
the raging sea which cannot rest, the waves
thereof cast up dirt and mire. There is
no peace to the wicked, saith the Lord
God.' But very different is it, as to the
things of God, for souls in grace. He who
loves God has perfect peace. As it is said
(Ps. cxviii. 165), 'Much peace have they
that love Thy law; and to them there is
no stumbling-block.' The reason of this
is that only God can satisfy the desire of
our souls; for He, as St. John says (1 Ep.
iii. 20), 'is greater than our heart.' Thus
St. Augustin says, in the first chapter of
his Confessions, 'Thou hast made us, O
Lord, for Thyself, and our hearts are restless till they rest in Thee.' David also says
(Ps. cii. 5), He 'satisfieth thy desire with
good things.'

5. **Dignity.** Charity confers a great dig-

nity on man. All things serve the majesty of God; for all things were made by Him, and things made serve their maker. But, to those who are slaves, charity gives freedom, making them the friends of God. So our Lord said to His Apostles (St. John xv. 15), 'I will not now call you servants, for the servant knoweth not what his Lord doeth. But I have called you friends; because all things whatsoever I have heard of My Father I have made known to you. You have not chosen Me, but I have chosen you.'

You will say, Was not St. Paul a servant? Did not other Apostles also write themselves servants? To that it is answered, We may be servants in two ways: *a.* in the way of fear; and, *b.* in the way of love.

a. Fear. The way of fear* is penal, and not meritorious. If any one keep from sin

---

* The Saint is speaking of fear 'servilely servile.' We see this from his use of the word 'only.'

only from fear of punishment, he cannot merit by that, and is still in servitude.

b. Love. The way of love is full of merit. If any one act, not from fear of justice, but for love of God, he does not act as a slave, but as a free man, for he acts voluntarily. Our Lord says, 'I will not call you servants.' Why does He say this? St. Paul gives us the answer (Rom. viii. 15). 'You have not received the spirit of bondage again in fear; but you have received the Spirit of adoption of sons, whereby we cry, Abba, Father.' So St. John says (1 Ep. iv. 18), 'Fear is not in charity; but perfect charity casteth out fear, because fear hath pain.' Now love fills us with delight.

6. **Sonship of God.** Charity not only gives us freedom, but actually makes us children; according to St. John's teaching (1 Ep. iii. 1), 'Behold what manner of charity the Father hath bestowed upon us, that we should be called and should be the sons of God.' A stranger becomes an adopted son, when he acquires a right of

inheritance. Now we acquire a right to the inheritance of God, that is, to everlasting life; for it is said (Rom. viii. 16, 17), 'The Spirit Himself giveth testimony to our spirit, that we are the sons of God, and, if sons, heirs also; heirs indeed of God and joint-heirs with Christ.' In another place (Wisd. v. 5) it is said, 'How are they numbered among the children of God!'

Prayers.

I.

O God, in Thee I live and without Thee I die. Thou givest me Thy Spirit that I may have life and may have it more abundantly. Keep my heart from love of earth and earthly things, and let my soul so cling to Thee that I may be one spirit with Thee. May pure love transfigure me, O my God, every day, more and more, into Thy likeness.

O Holy Ghost, give me strength to be faithful in keeping my Creator's command-

D

ments. Thou art my Creator. Make me ever prompt in obedience. Let me be ready to bear all things and to do all things for the sake of Jesus, whom I love.

Be to me, O adorable Trinity, a safeguard against every danger. I will love Thee, O Lord, my strength. Look down upon me from heaven and give me help. O my God, let me so love Thee that all things may work together for my good, and that hard things may be sweet for Thee and for Thy sake. Let me always long for Thee and always love the coming of Jesus. Give me, O Lord of love, a crown of life in the day of the appearing of my Lord.

II.

O Jesus, let Thy sin-destroying love dwell always in my soul. Thou, in Thy graciousness, dost forgive me again and again. Give me, dear Lord, true sorrow for my sins. The more that I love Thee, the more I must grieve when I offend Thee.

O Lord, lighten my heart with Thine own brightness and the brightness of Thy Spirit, that I may always know what to believe, what to do, and what to desire. Lead me, my Saviour, in the right way. Thou art my Judge and my King. Jesus, give me joy in God; and let my soul, loving and longing, rest in Him.

Jesus, give me peace in God. Thou hast promised great peace to those who keep Thy law. Not as the world giveth, O Lord, dost Thou give Thy peace to me. In God, and only in God, can my soul find rest. O Jesus, fill my desire with all good; fill my heart with God. Teach me, my Saviour, to understand the dignity of Thy friends, and to lift up my head in Thy freedom. Do Thou fill my soul with delight, because I am a child of God, baptised into Thy mystical body, oftentimes forgiven, sanctified by Thy Spirit, fed with the Bread of life. The Spirit of love, as Thy Apostle teaches us, gives witness with our spirit that we are God's children.

O Jesus, Eternal Son, help me to live
more worthily of Thy Father and my Father
who is in heaven.

CHAPTER III.

OF THE ATTAINMENT AND THE INCREASE OF CHARITY.

FROM what has been said, you see the
advantages of charity; and therefore, since
charity is so full of blessing, we should
strive most earnestly to gain it and keep it.

Remember, no one can have charity
from himself. It is the gift of God alone.
For this reason St. John says (1 Ep. iv. 10),
'Not as though we had loved God, but because He hath first loved us.' In truth,
God does not love us because He is first
loved by us; but it is His love for us that
kindles in our hearts the fire of love for
Him.

Remember also this: though all gifts

come from 'the Father of lights,' never-theless the gift of charity far surpasses the rest. For all gifts* can exist without charity and the Holy Ghost; but with charity the Holy Ghost is of necessity possessed. Hence St. Paul says (Rom. v. 5), 'The charity of God is poured forth in our hearts by the Holy Ghost, who is given to us.' There may be the gift of tongues or of knowledge or of prophecy without grace and the Holy Ghost.

I. Though charity is a gift of God, a certain disposition is required on our part that we may have it. (1.) Two things are specially needed for gaining charity, and (2.) two other things are needed for its increase after it has been gained.

(1.) **For gaining charity.** 1. *We must often hear the word of God.* This is clear from our own experience. If we hear good of a person, we begin to love him. So, hearing the words of God, we are inflamed with

---

* As is plain from the context, the Saint is speaking of graces, 'gratis datas.'

His love; as the Psalmist says (cxviii. 140),
'Thy word is strongly kindled and heated,*
and Thy servant hath loved it.' Again
(civ. 19), 'The word of the Lord inflamed
him.' The two disciples, on their way to
Emmaus, being on fire with the love of
God, said (St. Luke xxiv. 32), 'Was not
our heart burning within us, while He
spoke in the way and opened to us the
Scriptures?' We read of the preaching of
St. Peter (Acts x. 44), 'While Peter was
yet speaking these words, the Holy Ghost
fell on all them that heard the word.' Now
it often happens in sermons that they who
come with hard hearts are kindled to the
love of God by the word of preaching.

2. *We must have ceaseless thoughts of
God's goodness.* David says (Ps. xxxviii. 4),
'My heart grew hot within me; and in
my meditation a fire shall flame out.' If,
then, you wish to be filled with the love
of God, meditate on His gifts. Think of
His kindnesses that have been heaped upon

* Vulg. Vehementer ignitum.

you, the dangers from which you have been saved, and the everlasting happiness that He has promised. Hard, indeed, must be the heart that can think of such benefits and not be kindled with love. For this reason St. Augustin says, 'Hard is the heart of a man who not only refuses to give love, but does not wish even to repay it.' It is always the case that, as bad thoughts destroy the love of God, so good thoughts bring it, feed it, and strengthen it. Isaias therefore gives us this command (i. 16), 'Take away the evil of your thoughts from my eyes.' It is said again (Wisd. i. 3), 'Perverse thoughts separate from God.'

(2.) **For strengthening charity.** 1. *We must keep the heart free from things that are earthy.* The heart cannot be rightly borne different ways. No one can love both God and the world. Thus the more that our hearts are cut off from the love of earth, the more they will be rooted and grounded in the love of God. St. Augustin therefore says, 'The poison of charity is the

hope of gaining or keeping the gifts of the
world; but its nourishment is the lessen-
ing of cupidity. Its perfection is the dying out of cupidity, for cupidity is the root
of all evil. Whoever, therefore, wishes to
nourish the love of God, let him be very
careful in rooting out all these wrong desires.' Now cupidity is the love of getting
or keeping earthly things. The beginning
of the decrease of this feeling is the fear of
God; for He alone cannot be feared without love. To this end religious orders
have been ordained, in which and by which
the soul is drawn from the love of joys
that are earthly and corruptible, being raised
to the love of God, as is signified where it
is said (2 Mac. i. 22), 'The time came that
the sun shone out which was before in a
cloud.' The sun, that is, the intellect of
man, is in a cloud when it is given up to
the pleasures of earth; but it shines out
when it is lifted up and drawn away from
this earthy love. It is also said in the passage from the Machabees, 'There was a great

fire kindled, so that all wondered.' For then the soul shines forth, and the love of God grows in it greatly.

2. *We must be patient in suffering.* It is plain that our love is not lessened, but rather increased, by going through great sufferings for one whom we love. 'Many waters cannot quench charity; neither can the floods drown it' (Cantic. viii. 7). That is to say, love is not destroyed by many tribulations. As a workman loves the work most which has cost him most pains, so holy men, who bear great trials for God, are more rooted in His love. In like manner, the more that the faithful suffer for the sake of God, the more does His love lift them up above earthly desires. We read in Genesis (vii. 17), 'The waters increased, and lifted up the ark on high from the earth.' The waters here signify sorrow and pain; the ark signifies the soul of the just man, or the whole Church of God.

Prayer.

O Holy Ghost, give me Thy love, and give me strength to keep it and use it. Thou art sweet and mighty in all Thy gifts; but Thy greatest gift is charity. The love of God is shed abroad in our hearts by Thee, O Holy Ghost, who art given to us.

O Spirit of healing, let me be always diligent in listening to the word of God; for that word is a bright fire, and by it souls are kindled. The hearts of the two disciples burned within them when Jesus spoke to them by the way, and opened to them the Scriptures. Bless the words of all preachers, O Spirit of life, that by them many hard hearts may be softened, and many dark hearts kindled to the love of God.

Help me to think, O Blessed Spirit, as much as I can, of God. He has shown me boundless mercy; He has saved me from many dangers; He has promised me the beatitude of heaven. May I love Him for all that He has done, and for all that He has promised ; but may I love Him still more for Himself. Thou, O Holy Ghost, art God.

O sweet Spirit, cut my heart away from pleasures that perish in the using, so that it may cling more closely to Thee. No one can love God and the world at the same time. As love of the creature dies out in the soul, so the love of God brightens in it. O Spirit of light, be to me a sun of splendour, and drive far from my heart all darkened clouds and all shadows of gloom.

O my Sanctifier, my patient God, give me patience that I may bear all things for Thy love, and suffer all things according to Thy will. As we suffer, so shall we be glorified ; and as we carry the Cross, so shall we be crowned. This is the gift of Jesus, who sent Thee to His Church.

Bring me, O Spirit of love, to the company of those blessed ones who, having come out of the great tribulation, and having washed their robes in the Blood of the

Lamb, are for ever before the throne of God, serving Him day and night in His temple.

———

CHAPTER IV.

OF THE LOVE OF GOD.

BEFORE His Passion, our Lord, being asked by one of the scribes, a doctor of the law, which was the greatest and first commandment, answered (St. Mark xii. 30), 'Thou shalt love the Lord thy God with thy whole heart, and with thy whole soul, and with thy whole mind, and with thy whole strength.' Among all the commandments this is the most useful, the greatest, and the grandest. That can be seen at once, for in this commandment all the others are fulfilled.

I. For the perfect fulfilling of this command, four things are needed.

1. A ceaseless remembrance of the kindnesses of God. All that we have comes

from Him; whether it be outward things, or our bodies, or our souls. It is our duty, therefore, to use all creatures for His glory, and to love Him with a perfect heart. Very thankless must he be who does not love any one of whose kindnesses he thinks. Turning such thoughts over in his mind, David said, (1 Par. xxix. 14), 'All things are Thine; and we have given Thee what we have received at Thy hand.' Because of this it is said in his praise (Ecclus. xlvii. 10), 'With his whole heart he praised the Lord, and loved God that made him.'

2. **Meditation on the perfection of God.** Since God, as St. John says (1 Ep. iii. 20), 'is greater than our heart,' it follows that we do not give Him enough, even if we serve Him with our whole heart and with all our strength. So it is said in Ecclesiasticus (xliii. 30-37), 'What shall we be able to do to glorify Him? for the Almighty Himself is above all His works? The Lord is terrible and exceedingly great, and His power is admirable. Glorify the

Lord as much as ever you can, for He will yet far exceed, and His magnificence is wonderful. Blessing the Lord, exalt Him as much as you can, for He is above all praise. When you exalt Him put forth all your strength, and be not weary; for you can never go far enough. Who shall see Him and declare Him? And who shall magnify Him as He is from the beginning? There are many things hidden from us that are greater than these; for we have seen but a few of His works. But the Lord hath made all things, and to the godly He hath given wisdom.'

3. **Forsaking worldly things and earthly things.** We do a great injury to God if we equal anything to Him: as Isaias teaches (xl. 18), 'To whom then have you likened God? or what image will you make for Him?' Now we make creatures equal to God when we try to love the corruptible gifts of time together with Him. Besides, we thus try to do what is altogether impossible. Moreover, Isaias

says (xxviii. 20), 'The bed is straitened
so that one must fall out; and a short
covering cannot cover both.' Here the
Prophet likens the heart of man to a narrow bed and a short covering; for narrow
indeed is the human heart when compared
with God. You drive God out of your
souls when you receive into them anything that is alien from Him. For God
will no more bear with a partner in the
love of the soul than a man will put up
with a divided heart in his wife. Therefore God says of Himself (Ex. xx. 5), 'I
am the Lord thy God, mighty, jealous.'
It is His will that we should love nothing
as much as we love Him, and that we
should love nothing apart from Him.

4. **Constant avoidance of sin in every
way.** No one in mortal sin can love God.
Our Lord says (St. Matt. vi. 24), 'No man
can serve two masters. For either he will
hate the one or love the other, or he will
cleave to the one and despise the other.
You cannot serve God and mammon.' The

soul therefore that is in mortal sin cannot love God; but Ezechias loved Him who 'wept with great weeping.' He said (Isaias xxxviii. 3), 'I beseech Thee, O Lord, remember how I have walked before Thee in truth and with a perfect heart, and have done that which is good in Thy sight.' Elias said (3 Kings xviii. 21), 'How long do ye halt between two sides?' As one who halts inclines now this way and now that way, so a sinner goes on, now giving himself up to sin and now trying to seek for God. For this reason God says by the Prophet Joel (ii. 12), 'Now therefore saith the Lord, Be converted to Me with all your heart, in fasting and in weeping and in mourning.'

II. There are two kinds of men who sin against this command.

1. **The unguarded.** There are they who in avoiding one sin commit another. For instance, they guard against luxury and commit the sin of usury. Nevertheless they are condemned; for as St. James

teaches (ii. 10), 'Whosoever shall keep the whole law, but offend in one point, is become guilty of all.' Of these some one has said, 'It is an impious thing to hope for a half pardon from God.'

2. **Concealers of sin.** There are they who confess some sins and conceal others; or at any rate make parts of their confession to different priests. These persons do not merit; nay, rather, they sin; because they mean to deceive God, and because they make a division in the Sacrament of Penance. Of such David says (Ps. lxi. 9), 'Trust in Him, all ye congregations of people; pour out your hearts before Him.' Here he teaches that all sins must be revealed in confession.

III. It having been shown that man is bound to give himself to God, it must now be shown what offerings of himself a man ought to make. These offerings are four; that is to say, his heart, his soul, his mind, and his strength. Thus it is said (St. Mark xii. 30), 'Thou shalt love the Lord

E

thy God with thy whole heart, and with thy whole soul, and with thy whole mind, and with thy whole strength.'

1. **The heart: intention.** You must know that the intention is understood by the heart. The intention has such power that it draws all works to itself. Hence actions that are good in themselves become bad by a bad intention. Our Lord says (St. Luke xi. 34), 'The light of thy body is thy eye. If thy eye be single, thy whole body will be lightsome; but if it be evil, thy body also will be darksome.' He means this: If your intention be bad, the whole gathering of your good works will become dark. Besides, in every work our intention must be fixed on God: as St. Paul says (1 Cor. x. 31), 'Whether you eat or drink, or whatsoever else you do, do all to the glory of God.'

2. **The soul: a good will.** A good intention is not enough; there must be also a good will, which is signified by the soul. A man often acts fruitlessly, notwithstand-

ing his good intention, from the want of a good will. Thus he might steal to feed a poor man. Here there is a good intention, but the needful uprightness of will is wanting. No wicked deed is excused by a good intention. This is the teaching of St. Paul, who says (Rom. iii. 8), 'And not rather, as we are slandered and as some affirm that we say, let us do evil that there may come good ; whose damnation is just.' In truth, a good will is added to a good intention when the will is in agreement with the will of God. We daily pray for this, saying in our Lord's words (St. Matt. v. 10), 'Hallowed by Thy name. Thy kingdom come. Thy will be done on earth, as it is in Heaven.' So our Lord says in prophecy (Ps. xxxix. 8, 9), 'Behold I come : in the head of the book it is written of me that I should do Thy will: O my God, I have desired it ; and Thy law is in the midst of my heart.' Because of these reasons Jesus says, ' With thy whole soul :' for in Scripture the soul is often taken for

the will.   Thus (Heb. x. 38), ' If he withdraw himself he shall not please My soul :'
that is to say, he will not be in union with
God's will.

3. **The mind : understanding.** With a
good intention and a good will some sin
may yet be found in the understanding ;
and therefore the whole mind must be
given to God.   The Apostle says (2 Cor.
x. 5), ' Bringing into captivity every understanding unto the obedience of Christ.'
Here the sins of two classes of persons
have to be considered.

a. Sins of thought. There are many who
do not sin in deed, and yet constantly
dwell upon the thought of sin.   Against
them the Prophet says (Isaias i. 16),
' Wash yourselves ; be clean ; take away
the evil of your thoughts from my
eyes.'

b. Unbelief. There are others who,
trusting in their own wisdom, do not yield
assent to the faith.   Such persons do not
give their minds to God ; and for them

there is the warning (Prov. iii. 5), 'Lean not upon thy own prudence.'

4. **All our strength**. It is not enough unless we give all our powers and all our strength to God : as it is said in the Psalms (lviii. 10, 11), 'I will keep my strength for Thee, ... my God.'

a. There are some who use all their strength in sinning ; and thus show their power. Against them Isaias testifies (v. 22-24), 'Woe to you that are mighty to drink wine and stout men at drunkenness : that justify the wicked for gifts, and take away the justice of the just from him. Therefore, as the tongue of the fire devoureth the stubble and the heat of the flame consumeth it, so shall their root be as ashes and their bud shall go up as dust. For they have cast away the law of the Lord of hosts, and have blasphemed the word of the Holy One of Israel.'

b. There are others who show their power and their strength in injuring their neighbours ; whereas they ought to manifest their strength in helping them: as it is said (Prov. xxiv. 11.), 'Deliver them that are led to death; and those that are drawn to death forbear not to save.'

Thus you see that, if you are to love God as you ought to love Him, you must give Him your intention and your will and your mind and your strength.

Prayer.

O Saviour of the world, Thou hast told me to love God with my whole heart. With Thee, if Thou dost strengthen me, I can do all things; but without Thee I can do nothing. Thou, as Man, lifted up on the Cross, dost draw me to Thyself; and as God, on Thy throne of glory, Thou dost draw me to Thyself where Thou art lifted up in Heaven.

Keep in my mind always, dear Jesus, a remembrance of the gifts of Thy Father, that, as good gifts are His, so I may give back to Him what I have received from His hand.

Keep in my mind always, O Incarnate Word, a remembrance of the goodness of Thy Father; for He alone, with Thee and Thy Holy Spirit, in His sweetness and preciousness, can satisfy my soul. Teach me and help me, my Jesus, that I may always be able to say, 'My God and my all.'

O my Jesus, let me be crucified with Thee, and let me die to the world. Let me always glory in Thy cross of salvation; and do Thou, my Lord, always live in me. I will leave all that I can for Thee; and I will always be ready to give up whatsoever Thou willest to take from me. Enlarge the littleness of my heart, and fill it with God. O, how great is God! O, how little is my heart!

Give me, my Jesus, great loathing of sin, and great sorrow for the wrong that I have done. Let me always turn to Thee with my whole heart; and let me be transfigured daily to Thy likeness by the sweetness of Thy Spirit.

With a pure intention I turn to Thee,

my God; with a good will I offer my life
to Thee; with a right mind I give myself
into Thy captivity; and I long to have
my weakness crowned in Thy strength,
and my darkness glorified in Thy light.
Thy captivity is the freedom of God.

O Jesus, Son of the living God, lift me
up from the bondage of corruption into
the liberty of the glory of Thy Father's
children.   O my Lord and my love, I
count all things but loss for Thee.

CHAPTER V.

OF THE LOVE OF OUR NEIGHBOUR.

OUR Lord, being asked which was the
greatest commandment, gave two answers
to that one question. He said, 'Thou shalt
love the Lord thy God.'   That answer has
been already explained.   He also said
(St. Matt. xxii. 39), 'Thou shalt love thy
neighbour as thyself.'

I. As to the second answer, we must

bear in mind that he who keeps this commandment fulfils the whole law; as St. Paul teaches (Rom. xiii. 10), 'The love of our neighbour worketh no evil; love therefore is the fulfilling of the law.'

To the love of our neighbour we are led by four motives.

1. **The love of God.** St. John says (1 Ep. iv. 20), 'If any man say, I love God, and hateth his brother, he is a liar.' For clearly he is a liar who says that he loves any one, hating, at the same time, his children, who are his members. But all the faithful are children of God and members of Christ, whose Apostle says (1 Cor. xii. 27), 'Now you are the body of Christ and members of member.' He therefore who hates his neighbour does not love God.

2. **The command of God.** Jesus, when He was going away, gave to His disciples this command of love above all other commands (St. John xv. 12), 'This is My commandment, that you love one

another, as I have loved you;' and (ver.
17), 'These things I command you, that
you love one another.' No one therefore
keeps the law of God who hates his neighbour. Hence the love of our neighbour is
taken as a sign of our keeping the law of
God. Our Lord teaches us this truth
(St. John xiii. 35), 'By this shall all
men know that you are My disciples, if
you have love one for another.' He does
not say that His disciples shall be known
by raising the dead or by any outward
miracle. He says that the mark by which
they shall be known is the mark of brotherly love. So well did Blessed John
understand this truth, that he said (1 Ep.
iii. 14), 'We know that we have passed
from death to life, because we love the
brethren.' Why is this? He goes on to
tell us (ver. 14, 15), 'He that loveth not
abideth in death. Whosoever hateth his
brother is a murderer; and you know that
no murderer hath eternal life abiding in
him.'

3. **Our share in a like nature.** We read in Scripture (Ecclus. xiii. 19), 'Every beast loveth its like : so also every man him that is nearest to himself.' It follows then that men, being like in nature, are bound to love one another. It further follows that hatred of our neighbour is not only against the law of God, but also against the law of nature.

4. **The attainment of common benefits.** By charity the possessions of one person may be made useful to another. This it is which brings about the oneness of the Church and makes all things common, as David says (Ps. cxviii. 63), 'I am a partaker with all them that fear Thee, and keep Thy commandments.'

II. 'Thou shalt love thy neighbour as thyself.' This commandment about love of our neighbour is the second commandment (or the second table) of the law.* How much we have to love our neighbour has already been said. It remains for

* See the beginning of Chapter VI.

us to speak of the manner of that love which Jesus indicates, when He says, 'as thyself.' As to this, there are five points to be considered, by which we see the right way of loving our neighbour.

1. **We ought to love him truly as ourselves.** This we do if we love him for his own sake, and not for our sake. But here we must bear in mind that there are three kinds of love. Of these two are false, while the third is true.

a. There is a love which springs from selfishness. Holy Scripture says (Ecclus. vi. 10), 'There is a friend, a companion at the table, and he will not abide in the day of distress.' That plainly is not true love; for it fails when our advantage fails. In this case, therefore, we do not wish the good of our neighbour, but rather we wish for ourselves all that we can get.

b. There is another love which springs from what is pleasurable. This, however, cannot be true love; for when the pleasure ceases, the love ceases also. In this case we do not wish good to our neighbour chiefly for his own sake, but rather we desire his good for ourselves.

c. There is a third kind of love which springs from virtue. That is the only true love: for thus we love our neighbour for his own sake, and not for the sake of ourselves.

2. **We ought to love him in due order.** We are not to love him more than God or even as much as God; but we are to love him as ourselves. The Bride of Jesus says (Cantic. ii. 4), 'He set charity in order in me.' What this order is we learn from our Lord Himself (St. Matt. x. 37), 'He that loveth father or mother more than Me is not worthy of Me; and he that loveth son or daughter more than Me is not worthy of Me.'

3. **We ought to love him efficaciously;** that is, so as to do him some good. You do not only love yourselves, but you strive earnestly to get what is good for yourselves, and to avoid what is in any way hurtful to you. Thus also you should do to your

neighbour, according to the teaching of St. John (1 Ep. iii. 18), 'My little children, let us not love in word, nor in tongue, but in deed and in truth.' Certainly they are worst of all who love with their lips and hate with their hearts; for of these we read (Ps. xxvii. 3-5), 'Draw me not away with the wicked, and with the workers of iniquity destroy me not. For they speak peace with their neighbour, but evil is in their hearts. Give them according to their works, and according to the wickedness of their own inventions. According to the works of their hands give Thou to them; and render to them their reward. Because they have not understood the doings of the Lord, and the works of His hands, Thou shalt destroy them and not build them up.' St. Paul also warns us (Rom. xii. 9), 'Let love be without dissimulation; hating that which is evil; cleaving to that which is good.'

4. **We ought to love our neighbour always, as we love ourselves always.** The

Wise Man says (Prov. xvii. 17), 'He that is a friend loveth at all times; and a brother is proved in distress.' A friend is known and proved both in prosperity and adversity; but it is chiefly in adversity that his value is understood.

You should always bear in mind that there are two things which strengthen and preserve friendship.

a. The first is patience. In the Proverbs (xv. 17, 18) we read : 'It is better to be invited to herbs with love than to a fatted calf with hatred. A passionate man stirreth up strifes; he that is patient appeaseth those that are stirred up.'

b. The second is humility. Humility is the source and cause of patience. So we are taught in the Proverbs (xiii. 10), 'Among the proud there are always contentions ; but they that do all things with counsel are ruled by wisdom.' Any one who thinks a great deal of himself and looks down on another cannot bear that person's faults and failings.

5. **We must love him justly and ho-lily.** In other words, we must not love him with any reference to sin. We cannot rightly love ourselves in that way, for if we do we fall from God. In that way, therefore, we must not love our neighbour. Thus our Lord says to us (St. John xv. 9), 'As the Father hath loved Me, I also have loved you. Abide in My love.' Again it is said of that love (Ecclus. xxiv. 24), 'I am the mother of fair love.'

III. 'Thou shalt love thy neighbour as Thyself.' The Jews and the Pharisees understood this command wrongly. They thought that God commanded them to love their friends and hate their enemies. They therefore by 'neighbours' understood only their friends. But this mistake was con-demned by our Lord (St. Matt. v. 44-48), 'I say to you, Love your enemies; do good to them that hate you; and pray for them that persecute you and calumniate you, that you may be the children of your Father who is in heaven; who maketh His sun to rise upon the good and bad, and raineth upon the just and the unjust. For if you love them that love you, what reward shall you have? Do not even the publicans this? And if you salute your brethren only, what do you more? Do not also the heathen this? Be you therefore perfect, as your Heavenly Father is also perfect.' Besides, you must remember that he who hates his brother is not in a state of salvation. St. John warns us of this (1 Ep. ii. 11), 'He that hateth his brother is in darkness, and walketh in darkness, and knoweth not whither he goeth, because the darkness hath blinded his eyes.'

Here we see that there is an apparent contradiction to be explained; for there are those whom the good hate. David says (Ps. cxxxviii. 21, 22), 'Have I not hated them, O Lord, that hated Thee; and have I not pined away because of Thy enemies? I have hated them with a perfect hatred; and they are become enemies

F

to me.' So our Lord says in the Gospel
(St. Luke xiv. 26), 'If any man come to
Me and hate not his father and mother and
wife and children and brethren and sisters,
yea, and his own life also, he cannot be
My disciple.' To understand this we must
bear in mind that in all our doings the
deeds of our Lord are our examples. Now
God both loves and hates; for in every
man two things are to be considered, that
is, nature and sin. Nature indeed is worthy
of love in all men, but sin is worthy of
hatred. Hence, any one wishing another
to be in hell would hate nature; but wishing another to be good would hate sin;
and sin is always to be hated. For this
cause it is said in the Psalms (v. 6, 7),
' Neither shall the wicked dwell near Thee,
nor shall the unjust abide before Thy eyes.
Thou hatest all the workers of iniquity;
Thou wilt destroy all that speak a lie. The
bloody and the deceitful man the Lord will
abhor.' Again it is said (Wisd. xi. 25),
' Thou lovest all things that are, and hatest

none of the things which Thou hast made; for Thou didst not appoint or make anything, hating it.' Here you see that God loves and that God hates. He loves nature, but He hates sin. You also see that man, without sin, may sometimes inflict punishment, that is, when he does this for a good end; for God Himself acts in like manner. Thus He sends sickness; and they who were wicked in the days of their health are by that sickness converted to holiness. Again, He sends adversity, by which they are converted to good who aforetime in prosperity were bad. So Isaias teaches (xxviii. 19), 'Whensoever it shall pass through, it shall take you away; because in the morning early it shall pass through, in the day and in the night; and vexation alone shall make you understand what you hear.' Now we act in the same way, if we desire the punishment of a tyrant seeking to destroy the Church, in so far as we desire the good of the Church by the destruction of the tyrant. Hence it is said (2 Mac.

i. 17), 'Blessed be God in all things, who hath delivered up the wicked.' For this indeed all ought not only to wish, but also to work. There is no sin when the wicked are hanged by lawful authority. For St. Paul says (Rom. xiii. 1-5), 'Let every soul be subject to higher powers; for there is no power but from God; and those that are, are ordained of God. Therefore he that resisteth the power resisteth the ordinance of God; and they that resist, purchase to themselves damnation. For princes are not a terror to the good work, but to the evil. Wilt thou, then, not be afraid of the power? Do that which is good, and thou shalt have praise from the same; for he is God's minister to thee for good. But if thou do that which is evil, fear; for he beareth not the sword in vain; for he is God's minister, an avenger to execute wrath upon him that doeth evil. Wherefore be subject of necessity, not only for wrath, but for conscience-sake.' Such ministers of God as these do not depart from the law of love. Punishment, though sometimes for correction, is also sometimes for a good, better and more divine. Certainly the good of a whole city is greater than the life of one man. Only we must bear in mind that it is not enough for us not to wish the evil that is inflicted, we must also wish the good ; that is, not only improvement in the person punished, but also his eternal salvation. Now there are two ways in which we may wish good to another, that is, *a.* generally, and, *b.* specially.

a. Taken in the general way, we wish him good, as he is a creature of God and heir, if he please, of everlasting life.

b. In the special way, we wish him good, as he is our companion or friend.

From general love no one can be excluded ; for every one ought to pray for every one else, and ought also to help every one in the last extremity. You are not, however, bound to be on terms of familiarity with all unless they should ask pardon. If they do, then they are friends ; and if you refuse to forgive them, you hold friends in hatred. Hence our Lord says (St. Matt. vi. 14, 15), 'If you will forgive men their offences, your Heavenly Father will forgive you also your offences. But if you will not forgive men, neither will your Father forgive you your offences.' In His own prayer He teaches us to say (v. 12), 'Forgive us our debts, as we also forgive our debtors.'

IV. 'Thou shalt love thy neighbour as thyself.' It has been shown that you sin if you do not forgive one who asks for forgiveness, and that it is a part of perfection to draw such a one to yourself, even if you be not bound to do so. There are five reasons which would lead you thus to win him back.

1. **The preservation of proper dignity.** Diverse dignities have diverse signs, and no one can be allowed to cast away the signs of his own dignity. Now among all dignities the greatest is to be a son of God ;

and the sign of this dignity is to love your enemies; according to the teaching of Jesus (St. Matt. v. 44, 45), 'Love your enemies; do good to them that hate you; and pray for them that persecute and calumniate you: that you may be the children of your Father who is in heaven.' If you love a friend, that is no sign of the sonship of God; for Jesus tells you (v. 47) that even the heathen do this.

2. **A victory won.** This is what all men naturally desire. You must either draw the offender back to love by your kindness, and then you conquer, or he must draw you on to hatred, and then you are defeated. St. Paul sets this before us (Rom. xii. 21), ' Be not overcome by evil, but overcome evil by good.'

3. **The attainment of manifold usefulness.** By this you gain friends; according to the Apostle's teaching (Rom. xii. 20), ' If thy enemy be hungry, give him to eat; if he thirst, give him to drink; for doing this thou shalt heap coals of fire on his

head.' St. Augustin says, 'There is no greater incitement to love than to be before-hand in loving.' No one is so hard as to turn from that. We may refuse to give love, but we can hardly refuse to give it back. Thus (Ecclus. vi. 15), 'Nothing can be compared with a faithful friend, and no weight of gold and silver is able to countervail the goodness of his fidelity;' and again (Prov. xvi. 7), 'When the ways of man shall please the Lord, He will con-vert even his enemies to peace.'

4. **God will listen to your prayers more readily.** God once said by His prophet Jeremias (xv. 1), 'If Moses and Samuel shall stand before Me, My soul is not to-wards this people.' St. Gregory says of these words, 'He makes mention of Moses and Samuel before all others, because they prayed for their enemies.' In like manner Jesus Himself said (St. Luke xxiii. 34), 'Father, forgive them; for they know not what they do.' Blessed Stephen also prayed for his enemies, as his Master prayed (Acts

vii. 59) : 'Falling on his knees, he cried with a loud voice, saying, Lord, lay not this sin to their charge.' Great gain did he bring to the Church by this prayer, for he converted St. Paul.

5. **The avoidance of sin.** This we ought to desire with all the strength of our souls. Sometimes we sin and do not seek God; and then He draws us to Himself by sickness or other like trial. For this reason God says by Osee (ii. 6), 'Behold I will hedge up thy way with thorns, and I will stop it with a wall.' Thus Blessed Paul was drawn to God, according to that saying of the Psalmist (cxviii. 176), 'I have gone astray like a sheep that is lost; seek Thy servant :' and that other saying of the Bride (Cantic. i. 3), ' Draw me ; we will run after Thee to the odour of Thy ointments. The King hath brought me into His store-rooms ; we will be glad and rejoice in Thee.' We gain all this blessedness if we draw our enemy to ourselves by forgiving him first, as our Master teaches us

to do (St. Luke vi. 37, 38), ' Forgive, and you shall be forgiven. Give, and it shall be given to you : good measure and pressed down and shaken together and running over shall they give into your bosom. For with the same measure that you shall mete withal, it shall be measured to you again.' He also says (St. Matt. v. 7), ' Blessed are the merciful, for they shall obtain mercy.'

Now there is no greater mercy than the forgiveness of those who trespass against us.

Prayer.

My Jesus, Thou hast taught me to love God above all things, and Thou hast taught me to love my neighbour as myself. O Thou Lover of souls, O Thou Saviour of men, let me think over this, on my knees, before Thee.

Thou hast made all of us members of Thy mystical body. If, then, I do not love my brother I cannot love Thee, my elder Brother, who wast crucified for me ; and I

cannot love Thy Father who sent Thee;
nor Thy Spirit, whom Thou didst send.

After Thy last Supper, when the shadows
of the Passion were closing in upon Thee,
and Thy Soul was exceedingly sorrowful
even unto death, Thou hadst such a longing for love among Thy brethren that Thou
didst seem to take one commandment to
be Thy own above all others, saying to Thy
Apostles then, saying to us now, ' This is
My commandment, that ye love one another
as I have loved you.'

We are all of one flesh and one blood.
We all descend from Adam, whom Thou
didst make of the slime of the ground, and
from Eve, his wife, whom Thou didst make
of a rib taken from his side in the deep
sleep into which Thou hadst cast him.

Thy Church is one. Thinking of Thy
Apostles Thou didst speak of them to Thy
Father, and didst pray, saying, 'Not for
them only do I pray, but for them also who
through their word shall believe in Me;
that they all may be one, as Thou, Father,

in Me, and I in Thee, that they also may be one in Us.'

Give me grace, dear Jesus, to love my neighbour truly, not for my own advantage, nor for my own pleasure, but for his sake, and because it is Thy will. I desire always to do Thy will and have it in my heart. May I give my brethren a love that is duly ordered in Thee ; a love that will lead me to help them when I can, and to do them good. Let my deeds go with my words ; and let my tongue speak the truth. May this true affection from God be in my soul without change. May I love my brethren in justice and holiness ; and may I be patient and humble for Thy sake.

My Jesus, Thou hast said, 'Blessed are the merciful, for they shall obtain mercy.' Give me grace to forgive from my heart all those who in any way trespass against me. I pray now, dear Saviour, for all who have in any way injured me, and for all who in any way wish me evil or seek to do me harm.

CHAPTER VI.

OF THE FIRST COMMANDMENT OF THE LAW.

'THOU shalt not have strange gods before Me' (Ex. xx. 3). The whole law of Christ, as has already been shown, hangs on charity; while charity itself hangs on those two commands, of which one is about the love of God, and the other about the love of our neighbour.

We have considered these two commands, and we now go on to speak of the law which God gave to Moses. In giving that law, God gave him ten commandments, written on two tables of stone. Moses said to the children of Israel (Deut. v. 22), 'These words the Lord spoke to all the multitude of you in the mountain, out of the midst of the fire and the cloud and the darkness, with a loud voice, adding nothing more: and He wrote them in two tables of stone which He delivered unto me.' The three commandments written on the first table pertain to the love of

God; but the seven written on the second
table pertain to the love of our neighbour.
Thus the whole law is founded on these
two commandments.

Now we must love God, in our hearts,
in our lips, in our works. First, we must
love Him in heart. It is therefore said,
'Thou shalt not have strange gods before
Me.' Secondly, we must love Him in our
words. It is therefore said, 'Thou shalt
not take the name of the Lord thy God in
vain.' Thirdly, we must love Him in our
deeds. It is therefore said, 'Remember
that thou keep holy the Sabbath-day.'
(These are the three commandments about
God Himself. The Angelic Doctor speaks
of the second and third in the seventh and
eighth chapters. He goes on to speak of
the first now.)

I. The first commandment about the way
in which we are to love God is this,
'Thou shalt not have strange gods before
Me.'

To understand this command we must

call to mind four ways in which the ancient nations transgressed it.

1. **Some of them worshipped devils.** We read (Ps. xcv. 5), 'All the gods of the Gentiles were devils.' That was a fearful sin, and indeed the greatest of all sins. But even now there are many who break this commandment; that is to say, all those who use divinations or casting of lots. For these things, according to St. Augustin, cannot be done without leading us into some kind of bargain with the devil. Hear St. Paul (1 Cor. x. 20), 'The things which the heathen sacrifice they sacrifice to devils, and not to God. I would not that you should be made partakers with devils.' Then he adds (v. 21), 'You cannot drink the chalice of the Lord and the chalice of devils. You cannot be partakers of the table of the Lord and of the table of devils.'

2. **Others worshipped the heavenly bodies.** They believed that the stars were gods: as we read in the Book of Wisdom (xiii. 2), 'They have imagined the fire, or

the wind, or the swift air, or the circle of stars, or the great water, or the sun and moon to be the gods that rule the world.' They thought that the sun and moon were rulers of the whole earth, and that thus they were gods; and therefore Moses forbade the Jews to lift their eyes to the sun and moon in the way of adoring them (Deut. iv. 15, 19), 'Keep, therefore, your souls carefully, .. lest, perhaps, lifting up thy eyes to heaven thou see the sun and the moon and all the stars of heaven; and being deceived by error thou adore and serve them, which the Lord, thy God, created for the service of all the nations under heaven.'

Astrologers sin against this commandment, for they say that heavenly bodies are the rulers of souls; whereas, we know that they were all made for man, and that man's only ruler is God.

3. **Others worshipped the lower elements.** They believed the wind and fire to be gods, as we have seen in the verse of the Book of Wisdom just quoted. There

are men still who fall into this error; for all sin in this way who use creatures badly by loving them too much. St. Paul warns us about this sin very strongly (Eph. v. 5), 'Know ye this and understand that no fornicator or unclean or covetous person, which is a serving of idols, hath inheritance in the kingdom of Christ and of God.'

4. **Men also fell into error and sin by worshipping birds or other men or themselves.** This came about for a threefold reason.

a. From a carnal mind. It is said (Wisd. xiv. 15, 16, 21), 'A father being afflicted with bitter grief made to himself the image of his son who was quickly taken away: and him who then had died as a man he began now to worship as a god, and appointed him rites and sacrifices among his servants. Then, in process of time, wicked custom prevailing, this error was kept as a law, and statues were worshipped by the command of tyrants. . . . This was the occasion of deceiving human life; for

G

men, serving either their affection or their kings, gave the incommunicable Name to stones and wood.'

b. From a spirit of flattery. It is said (Wisd. xiv. 17), 'Those whom men could not honour in presence because they dwelt far off, they brought in resemblance from afar ; and made an express image of the king whom they had a mind to honour : that, by this their diligence, they might honour as present him that was absent.' This they did by making images of them, and then worshipping the images in their stead.   Such as these are all they who love and worship men more than they love and worship God.   Our Lord says, as we have seen before (St. Matt. x. 37), 'He that loveth father or mother more than Me is not worthy of Me: and he that loveth son or daughter more than Me is not worthy of Me !'   There is also the warning of the Psalmist (cxlv. 2, 3.), 'Put not your trust in princes ; in the children of men in whom there is no salvation.'

c. From presumption. Some in a like spirit have actually set themselves up as gods. We read (Judith iii. 13), 'Nabuchodonosor the king had commanded him to destroy all the gods of the earth, that he only might be called god by those nations which could be brought under him by the power of Holofernes.' Ezechiel tells us of the prince of Tyre (xxviii. 2, 6-8), 'Thus saith the Lord God, Because thy heart is lifted up and thou hast said, I am god, and I sit in the seat of God in the heart of the sea ; whereas thou art a man and not God ; and hast set thy heart as if it were the heart of God : . . . therefore thus saith the Lord God, Because thy heart is lifted up as the heart of God, behold I will bring upon thee strangers, the strongest of the nations ; and they shall draw their swords against the beauty of thy wisdom, and they shall defile thy beauty. They shall kill thee and bring thee down ; and thou shalt die the death of them that are slain in the heart of the sea.'

Like these men in their works are all they who follow their own senses more than the commands of God : for thus truly they worship themselves as God. Following the delights of the flesh, they worship their bodies instead of God. Of these St. Paul speaks (Phil. iii. 18, 19), ' Many walk, of whom I have told you often, and now tell you weeping, that they are the enemies of the Cross of Christ ; whose end is destruction ; whose god is their belly ; whose glory is in their shame ; who mind earthly things.' Against sins, such as these, therefore, you must be very carefully on your guard.

II. ' Thou shalt not have other gods before Me.' By the first commandment of the law we are forbidden to worship any god but the one true and only God. To keep this command we are drawn by five motives.

1. **By the greatness and majesty of God.** If the majesty of God be lessened by us in any way, we do Him an injury. This you see even from the manners and

customs of men. Due honour has to be given to each person according to his dignity. Hence a man is counted a traitor who takes away from the king that which he is bound to give. So we are traitors to God if we do not give Him all that is His due. Listen to St. Paul (Rom. i. 21-23), 'When they knew God they have not glorified Him as God, nor given thanks, but they became vain in their thoughts, and their foolish heart was darkened. For professing themselves to be wise they became fools; and changed the glory of the incorruptible God into the likeness of the image of a corruptible man, and of birds, and of four-footed beasts, and of creeping things.' This guilt, above every other guilt, brings on them the anger of God, who has said (Is. xlviii. 11), 'For My own sake, for My own sake, will I do it, that I may not be blasphemed, and I will not give My glory to another.' Again (Is. xlii. 8), 'I, the Lord, this is My name ; I will not give My glory to another, nor My praise to graven things.'

We must bear in mind that the majesty of God is in His omniscience. There is nothing which He does not know; and this knowledge is one sign of Godhead, as Isaias teaches (xli. 23), 'Show the things that are to come hereafter, and we shall know that ye are gods;' and as St. Paul also teaches, (Heb. iv. 13), 'Neither is there any creature invisible in His sight; but all things are naked and open to His eyes.'

Soothsayers or fortune-tellers take away from this majesty of God, and against them Isaias testifies (viii. 19), 'When they shall say to you, Seek of pythons and of diviners who mutter in their enchantments, should not the people seek of their God? (Should they not seek) from the living of the dead?'

2. **By the bountifulness of God.** We have all our good from God. Nay, it pertains to the majesty of God that He should be the doer of all good and the giver of all good. So the Psalmist witnesses of Him (ciii. 24, 27, 28), 'How great are Thy works, O Lord; Thou hast made all things

in wisdom; the earth is filled with Thy riches. ... All wait on Thee, and Thou givest them food in due season. What Thou givest to them they shall gather up; when Thou openest Thy hand they shall all be filled with good.' God is the giver of all gifts, filling all things with the richness of His goodness. Thankless, therefore, exceedingly, art thou if thou dost not acknowledge the benefits that He heaps upon thee. Still more thankless art thou if thou make for thyself another god, as the children of Israel, when they were brought safely out of Egypt, made for themselves a golden calf. Sinners, such as these, say (Osee ii. 5), 'I will go after my lovers;' and according to the words of the Prophet they shall be 'covered with shame.'

Again, they commit the same sin who set their hope in creatures more than in God, or who seek for help from any one but Him. So David tells us (Ps. xxxix. 5), 'Blessed is the man whose trust is in the name of the Lord, and who hath not had

regard to vanities and lying follies.' St.
Paul also warns us (Gal. iv. 9-11), 'Now,
after that you have known God, or rather
are known by God, how turn you again to
the weak and needy element which you
desire to serve again? You observe days
and months and times and years. I am
afraid of you, lest perhaps I have laboured
in vain among you.'

3. **By faithfulness to our promise.** We
have renounced the devil, and we have
plighted our faith to God alone. As we
have made Him this promise we ought not
to break it. Indeed if we do we bring
great punishment on ourselves. We have
a warning in the Epistle to the Hebrews
(x. 28-31), 'A man making void the law of
Moses dieth without any mercy under two
or three witnesses; how much more do you
think he deserveth worse punishments, who
hath trodden underfoot the Son of God, and
hath counted the blood of the covenant
unclean, by which he was sanctified, and
hath offered an affront to the Spirit of

grace? For we know Him that hath said, Vengeance belongeth to Me and I will repay; and again, The Lord shall judge His people. It is a fearful thing to fall into the hands of the living God.' To the faithless soul we may apply the words of St. Paul (Rom. vii. 3), 'While her husband liveth she shall be called an adultress, if she be with another man;' and of Thamar, Juda said (Gen. xxxviii. 24), 'Bring her out that she may be burnt.' (The holy Baptist tells us what our Lord will do (St. Luke iii. 16, 17), 'He shall baptise you with the Holy Ghost and with fire; whose fan is in His hand, and He will purge His floor; and will gather the wheat into His barn, but the chaff He will burn with unquenchable fire.' St. John says of Babylon, that is, the faithless soul (Apoc. xviii. 8), 'Her plagues shall come in one day, death and mourning and famine, and she shall be burned with the fire; because God is strong who shall judge her.')

Woe, therefore, to the sinner who 'goeth

two ways' (Ecclus. iii. 28), and to those
who are ever 'halting between two sides'
(3 Kings xviii. 21). So it is written
(Ecclus. ii. 14), 'Woe to them that are of
a double heart, and to wicked lips, and to
the hands that do evil, and to the sinner
that goeth on the earth two ways.'

4. **By the bitterness of the slavery of
the devil.** Jeremias threatens (xvi. 13) :
' I will cast you forth out of this land into
a land which you know not, nor your
fathers ; and there you shall serve strange
gods, day and night, which shall not give
you any rest.' For the soul does not stop
at one sin ; but rather it strives to go from
sin to sin. Our Lord warns us (St. John
viii. 34) : ' Amen, amen, I say to you, that
whosoever committeth sin is the servant of
sin.' This being so, it is not an easy thing
for a man to leave the bondage of sin. St.
Gregory says, ' The sin, which is not washed away by penance, drags the soul to
other sins by its own weight.'

Very different from slavery like this is

the divine yoke of Jesus. Of Him St. John says (1 Ep. v. 3), 'His commandments are not heavy.' So He says of Himself (St. Matt. xi. 28-30), 'Come to Me, all you that labour and are burdened, and I will refresh you. Take My yoke upon you and learn of Me, because I am meek and humble of heart, and you shall find rest for your souls. For My yoke is sweet, and My burden light.'

Indeed, if a man would only do as much for God as he has done for sin, that would be counted enough. St. Paul shows us this (Rom. vi. 19), 'As you have yielded your members to serve uncleanness, and iniquity unto iniquity, so now yield your members to serve justice unto sanctification.'

On the other hand, of the servants of the devil, it is written (Wisd. v. 7), 'We wearied ourselves in the way of iniquity and destruction, and have walked through hard ways, and the way of the Lord we have not known.' So Jeremias witnesses

(ix. 5), 'They have laboured to commit iniquity.'

5. **By the greatness of the reward.** Here is the greatness of the gift of God. In no law are there promises like the promises of the law of Christ. The Jews looked forward to the land of promise flowing with milk and honey; but Christians wait for the glory of the angels. Jesus said (St. Matt. xxii. 30), 'In the resurrection they . . . shall be as the angels of God in heaven.' When St. Peter thought of this, he said to Jesus (St. John vi. 69), 'Lord, to whom shall we go? Thou hast the words of eternal life.'

Prayer.

O adorable Trinity, one God, uncreated, everlasting; Thou art my God, and I bless Thee; Thou art my God, and I praise Thee; Thou art my God, and I love Thee with all my heart. I have no God but Thee, my own God; for Thou didst make me. For Thyself Thou didst make me. I love Thee very little ; but I long to love Thee more. I desire, with a great desire, to have Thee dwelling in my soul. O Fountain of life, be to me all in all. O great Reward, be to me the fulness of my desire. My heart leaps up for joy when I remember that I come from Thee, and that, if I be faithful, I shall go back to Thee at the last.

O adorable Trinity, I bow down before the majesty of Thy glory and Thy splendour in the inaccessible light. With seraphim and cherubim I veil the eyes of my soul before the greatness of Thy white throne. Like a flame of living fire Thy train is filling all the temple.

O adorable Trinity, I bow down before Thy goodness and the bountifulness of Thy love. Unsearchable riches are ever flowing from Thee in the kingdom of nature, and far more unsearchable riches in the kingdom of grace. O, how blessed are all souls that have a hope of seeing Thee and possessing Thee for ever ! O Blessed Trinity, give me always a heart of thankfulness, and give me at last the possession of Thyself.

My God, I have promised to be faithful to Thee : give me grace to keep my promise. Thou never leavest me, never forsakest me. Thy watchful eyes are always over me, and Thy ears are open to my prayers. Thou art the keeper of my soul, and Thou neither slumberest nor sleepest.

Keep before my eyes, O Blessed Trinity, the brightness of Thy reward. Eye hath not seen and ear hath not heard the things that Thou hast promised to give us. Thou dost reveal them by Thy Spirit. Thy word is truth. I am looking onward for the day when, with Thy angels, I shall praise Thee for ever. In Thy light I shall see light.

O most Blessed Trinity, great and precious are Thy promises and Thy rewards; but, O my God, Thou art Thyself far more than all. Countless worlds of love and light and beauty would be nothing compared with Thee. O adorable Trinity, Well-spring of living waters, Thou art the God of my heart, and I have no God but Thee.

CHAPTER VII.

OF THE SECOND COMMANDMENT OF THE LAW.

'THOU shalt not take the name of the Lord thy God in vain' (Ex. xx. 7). This is the second commandment of the law. As there is only one God whom we can worship, so there is only one God whom we venerate in the highest way. We are therefore commanded not to take His name in vain.

I. We must first understand that the word 'vain' is taken in a threefold sense.

1. **Sometimes it means a lie.** We read in the Psalms (xi. 3), 'They have spoken vain things, every one to his neighbour; with deceitful lips and with a double heart have they spoken.' You, therefore, take God's name in vain when you use it to

confirm a lie. Zacharias says (viii. 17), 'Love not a false oath;' and he adds in another place (xiii. 3), 'Thou shalt not live, because thou hast spoken a lie in the name of the Lord.'

A man who acts in this way does injury, *a.* to God; *b.* to himself; *c.* to all other men.

a. He does injury to God. To swear by God is nothing else but to call Him to be a witness. When therefore you swear to a lie, you seem to think that God (*a.*) does not know the truth; or (*b.*) loves a lie; or (*c.*) has little power.

(*a.*) In the first case you make Him out to be ignorant, though (Heb. iv. 13) 'all things are naked and open to His eyes.'

(*b.*) In the second case you deny the witness of Holy Scripture about His hatred of falsehood (Ps. v. 7), 'Thou wilt destroy all that speak a lie.'

(*c.*) In the third case you derogate from His power, as if He could not bear witness, or as if He could not punish.

b. He does injury to himself. He binds himself by the judgment of God. To call God thus to witness is nothing else than to say, ' May God punish me, if this be not so.'

c. He does injury to others. No society could last among men if they did not trust one another. If the facts be doubted, then they are confirmed by an oath, as it is said (Heb. vi. 16), 'Men swear by one greater than themselves, and an oath for confirmation is the end of all their controversy.'

A man, therefore, who swears falsely, *a.* does an injury to God; *b.* is cruel to himself; *c.* is a pest to his neighbours.

2. **Sometimes ' vain' is taken for useless.** We read in the Psalms (xciii. 11), ' The Lord knoweth the thoughts of men, that they are vain.' Thus God's name is taken in vain when we use it about frivolous matters. In the old law men were forbidden to swear uselessly (Deut. v. 11): ' Thou shalt not take the name of the Lord thy God in vain: for he shall not be un-

H

punished that taketh His name upon a vain thing.' But our Lawgiver forbade us to swear, save in case of necessity (St. Matt. v. 33-37) : 'You have heard that it was said to them of old, Thou shalt not forswear thyself, but thou shalt perform thy oaths to the Lord. But I say unto you, Not to swear at all: neither by heaven, for it is the throne of God; nor by the earth, for it is His footstool; nor by Jerusalem, for it is the city of the great King. Neither shalt thou swear by thy head, because thou canst not make one hair white or black. But let your speech be yea, yea; no, no; and that which is over and above these is of evil.'

Jesus spoke in this way because in no part are we so frail as in our tongue. Hear St. James (iii. 2) : 'If any man offend not in word, he is a perfect man.' So again (vv. 7, 8), 'Every nature of beasts, and of birds, and of serpents, and of the rest is tamed, and hath been tamed by the nature of man; but the tongue no man can tame, an unquiet evil, full of deadly poison.' Very easily, therefore, may a man swear falsely ; and for this reason our Lord says, as we have just seen, ' Let your speech be yea, yea ; no, no.' ' I say unto you, Not to swear at all.'

You should observe that an oath is like medicine : it is not always taken, but only in case of necessity. Therefore our Lord says (St. Matt. v. 37), ' That which is over and above these is of evil.' So the Scriptures warn us (Ecclus. xxiii. 9) : ' Let not thy mouth be accustomed to swearing, for in it there are many falls.' Again (vv. 12-14), ' A man that sweareth much shall be filled with iniquity, and a scourge shall not depart from his house. . . . If he swear in vain he shall not be justified : for his house shall be filled with his punishment.' Again (v. 10), ' Let not the naming of God be usual in thy mouth, and meddle not with the names of saints, for thou shalt not escape free from them.'

3. **Sometimes 'vain' is taken for sin or injustice.** We read in the Psalms (iv. 3)

' O ye sons of men, how long will ye be dull of heart? Why do ye love vanity, and seek after lying?' He therefore who swears towards the commission of sin takes the name of God in vain.

Now the two parts of justice are, *a.* to do good, and, *b.* to forsake evil.

a. If therefore you swear that you will steal or commit any other sin, you sin against justice. Though an oath like that must not be kept, nevertheless he who takes it is a perjurer. In the case of the Holy Baptist, Herod was such a perjurer as this (St. Mark vi. 23) : ' He swore to her, Whatsoever thou shalt ask, I will give it thee, though it be the half of my kingdom.'

b. In like manner he sins against justice who swears that he will not do something that is good. For instance, he may swear not to enter a church or not to become a religious. Such oaths as these must not be kept; but nevertheless he who takes them is a perjurer.

Therefore you must never swear, 1. falsely, nor, 2. uselessly, nor, 3. unjustly. The prophet Jeremias tells us what to do (iv. 2) : 'Thou shalt swear, As the Lord liveth, in truth and in judgment and in justice.'

4. **Sometimes 'vain' is taken for the height of folly.*** Thus it is written (Wisd. xiii. 1), ' All men are vain in whom there is not the knowledge of God.' They therefore who use God's name recklessly, as blasphemers do, take that name in vain. Of such men the law of Moses decreed (Lev. xxiv. 16), 'He that blasphemeth the name of the Lord dying, let him die.'

---

* St. Thomas uses the word 'fatuus,' and that is a stronger word than ' stultus,' the fool. Cicero classes the 'fatuus' man with the ' amens,' or one who acts as if he were mad. 'Non modo nequam et improbus sed etiam fatuus et amens es.' We have the word in 'infatuation,' but that does not express the meaning fully. Perhaps ' recklessly' comes as near to it as anything else. At any rate we can easily see the Saint's meaning, when he puts blasphemy among such kinds of folly.

II. 'Thou shalt not take the name of the Lord thy God in vain.' You must now learn that there are six ways in which we can rightly use the name of God.

1. **To confirm what we say, as in an oath.** By this we acknowledge that the purest truth is in God, and only in Him; and so by this we show reverence to God. Hence there was in the law this command (Deut. vi. 13), 'Thou shalt fear the Lord thy God, and shalt serve Him only, and thou shalt swear by His name.' They who swear in any other way dishonour God; and therefore it is said (Ex. xxiii. 13), 'By the name of strange gods you shall not swear; neither shall it be heard out of your mouth.' Though sometimes a person may swear by creatures, yet that is in reality by God. If, for instance, you swear by your head or your soul, you mean to bind yourself by punishments of God. Thus St. Paul (2 Cor. i. 23), 'I call God to witness on my soul.' So if you swear on the Gospels, you swear by God who

gave the Gospels. It is a sin, therefore, when men swear too readily by God or by the Gospels.

2. **For sanctification.** We know from St. Paul that baptism sanctifies us (1 Cor. vi. 11) : 'Such some of you were; but you are washed, but you are sanctified, but you are justified, in the name of our Lord Jesus Christ and the Spirit of our God.' Now baptism has its power only by the invocation of the Holy Trinity; and therefore it is said by Jeremias (xiv. 9), 'Thou, O Lord, art among us, and Thy name is called upon by us; forsake us not.'

3. **To drive away the enemy.** Before baptism the devil is renounced. To this we may apply the words of Isaias (iv. 1): 'Only let us be called by Thy name; take away our reproach.' A baptised soul therefore going back into sin takes God's name in vain.

4. **For an acknowledgment of the name of God.** St. Paul asks (Rom. x. 14), 'How shall they call on Him in whom they

have not believed ?' Again, he says (v. 13),
'Whosoever shall call upon the name of
the Lord shall be saved.'

But we confess God in two ways : *a.* by
our lips, and, *b.* by our works.

*a. When we confess Him by our lips we
manifest His great glory.* Hence it is said
by Isaias (xliii. 7), ' Every one that calleth
upon My name, I have created him for My
glory ; I have formed him and made him.'
If therefore you say anything against the
glory of God, you take His name in vain.

*b. We confess Him by our works when we
do those things which set forth His glory.*
Jesus says (St. Matt. v. 16), ' So let your
light shine before men that they may see
your good works, and glorify your Father
who is in heaven.'   But there are men
who do the contrary, and of them St. Paul
says (Rom. ii. 24), ' The name of God
through you is blasphemed among the
Gentiles.'

5. **For a safeguard and defence.**   So
in Proverbs (xviii. 10), ' The name of the

Lord is a strong tower; the just runneth
to it, and shall be exalted.' Again (St.
Mark xvi. 17), 'In My name they shall
cast out devils.' Again, 'Peter, filled with
the Holy Ghost, said to them' (Acts iv.
10-12), 'Be it known to you all and to all
the people of Israel, that by the name of
our Lord Jesus Christ of Nazareth, whom
you crucified, whom God hath raised from
the dead, even by Him this man standeth
here before you, whole. This is the stone
which was rejected by you, the builders,
which is become the head of the corner.
Neither is there salvation in any other;
for there is no other name under heaven
given to men whereby we must be saved.'

6. **For the fulfilling of our work.** We
have the teaching of St. Paul (Col. iii. 17),
'All, whatsoever you do in word or in
work, all things do ye in the name of the
Lord Jesus Christ, giving thanks to God
and the Father by Him.' It is the teaching also of the Psalms (cxxiii. 8), 'Our
help is in the name of the Lord, who

made heaven and earth.' Sometimes, however, as for instance in the case of an unfulfilled vow, a person begins imprudently. Such a one takes God's name in vain. Hence the Preacher says (Eccles. v. 1, 3), 'Speak not anything rashly, and let not thy heart be hasty to utter a word before God. For God is in heaven and thou upon earth; therefore let thy words be few. . . . If thou hast vowed anything to God, defer not to pay it; for an unfaithful and foolish promise displeaseth Him.'

Prayer.

Glorious and venerable is Thy name, O God; and that my soul knoweth right well. In Thy Godhead Thou art one; in Thy Persons Thou art three; Thou art without beginning and without end. I love Thy incommunicable name; and I will praise it and magnify it for ever.

Give me grace, O God, to glorify Thee by the truthfulness of my life and by the truthfulness of my lips. By Thy grace I will always hate all falsehood and lying with a great hatred, according to the divine hatred that is in Thee. O my God, Thou art adorable in Thy hatred of evil, as Thou art adorable in Thy love of good. By Thy help I will turn away from all kinds of lying, and, most of all, from that worst kind of lying which is calling Thee, O Thou God of justice, to bear witness to the truth of a lie.

Set a watch, O Lord, upon my tongue, and keep the door of my lips. I know how often I offend Thee by my words. Day by day I make resolutions against sinning by word, and often I fall into those very sins. It is my own fault, O God of truth, it is my own most grievous fault, because I trust too much to myself and too little to Thee. Yet one thing I may gain from my falls. I learn, step by step, to understand my own weakness and the might of Thy upholding arm.

O God, most gracious and most loving, let me glorify Thy name in my heart, in

my lips, and in my deeds. Save me from
all falsehood of injustice, and save me from
all blasphemy against Thy adorable name.
By Thy name I am made strong, and in
Thy name I will trust. I will praise Thy
name and exalt it, and magnify it for ever.
Thou art merciful, long-suffering, patient,
pitiful, and very compassionate. I adore
Thy venerable name.

Let the light of Thy name, O God, lie
for evermore in my heart like the splendour of seven days.

CHAPTER VIII.

OF THE THIRD COMMANDMENT OF THE LAW.

'REMEMBER that thou keep holy the Sabbath-day' (Ex. xx. 8). We come now to
the third commandment of the law. There
is great fittingness in this order; for, as
we have seen,* we honour God with the

* See the beginning of Chapter VI.

heart, with the lips, and by our works. In what has been said of the first two commandments we learn how to honour Him in heart and lips. Now, that we may know how to honour Him in deeds, it is said, 'Remember that thou keep holy the Sabbath-day.'

I. God willed that there should be a fixed day on which men should specially give themselves up to serving Him. This command, therefore, was given for five reasons.

1. **For the uprooting of error.** The Holy Ghost foresaw how in the coming days there would be found men to say that the world had always existed. For this we have the word of St. Peter (2 Ep. iii. 3-5): 'Knowing this first, that in the last days there shall come deceitful scoffers walking after their own lusts, saying, Where is His promise or His coming? for since the time that the fathers slept, all things continue as they were from the beginning of the creation. For this they are

wilfully ignorant of, that the heavens were before, and the earth out of water and through water, consisting by the word of God.' It was therefore the will of God that one day should be kept sacred in memory of His creating all things in six days, and resting on the seventh day from the new work that He had made. God Himself gives this reason in the law, for He says (Ex. xx. 8-11), 'Remember that thou keep holy the Sabbath-day. Six days shalt thou labour, and do all thy works; but on the seventh day is the Sabbath of the Lord thy God. Thou shalt do no work on it; thou, nor thy son, nor thy daughter, nor thy man-servant, nor thy maid-servant, nor thy beast, nor the stranger that is within thy gates. For in six days the Lord made heaven and earth, and the sea, and all things that are in them, and rested on the seventh day. Therefore the Lord blessed the seventh day, and sanctified it.'

The Jews kept the Sabbath in memory of the first creation; but our Lord, at His coming, made a new creation. By the first creation man is of the earth; but by the second creation he is of heaven: as St. Paul says (Gal. vi. 15), 'In Christ Jesus neither circumcision availeth anything, nor uncircumcision, but a new creature.' The new creature is made by grace, and the grace began in the resurrection. So St. Paul teaches (Rom. vi. 4-9), 'We are buried together with Him by baptism unto death; that as Christ is risen from the dead by the glory of the Father, so we also may walk in newness of life. For if we have been planted together in the likeness of His death, we shall be also in the likeness of His resurrection ; knowing this, that our old man is crucified with Him that the body of sin may be destroyed, to the end that we may serve sin no longer. For he that is dead is justified from sin. Now if we be dead with Christ we believe that we shall live also together with Christ; knowing that Christ rising from the dead dieth no more ; death shall no more have dominion over Him.' The resurrection, then, having taken place on a Sunday, we keep that day holy, as the Jews kept the Sabbath holy because of the first creation.

2. **For the gift of an instructed faith in our Redeemer.** The flesh of Jesus was not corrupted in the grave. It is said in the Psalms (xv. 9), 'My heart hath been glad, and my tongue hath rejoiced; moreover My flesh also shall rest in hope.' In the same place also it is said (v. 10), 'Thou wilt not leave My soul in hell; nor wilt Thou give Thy holy one to see corruption.' For this reason God willed the Sabbath to be kept that, as the sacrifices of the law signified the death of Christ, so the rest of the Sabbath might signify the rest of His flesh. We do not offer those sacrifices now; for, as is fitting, the type ceases when the reality and the truth have come; just as the shadows flee away at the rising of the sun. But we keep Saturday holy in honour of the glorious Virgin in whose soul, on that day, the

faith burned brightly during the death of the Incarnate Word.

3. **To strengthen the promise or to be a type of it.** God has promised us rest. Isaias says (xiv. 3, 4, 7), 'It shall come to pass in that day, that when God shall give thee rest from thy labour and from thy vexation and from the hard bondage wherewith thou didst serve before, thou shalt take up this parable against the king of Babylon, and shalt say, How is the oppressor come to nothing ; the tribute hath ceased. . . The whole earth is quiet and still ; it is glad and hath rejoiced.' Again he says (xxxii. 17, 18), 'The work of justice shall be peace, and the service of justice quietness and security for ever ; and My people shall sit in the beauty of peace and in the tabernacles of confidence and in wealthy rest.'

Remember that we look for rest from three things : *a.* from the sufferings of this life ; *b.* from the pain of temptations ; *c.* from the slavery of the devil. All this

I

Jesus promised to those who will come to Him (St. Matt. xi. 28-30): 'Come to Me, all ye that labour and are burdened; and I will refresh you. Take My yoke upon you, and learn of Me, for I am meek and humble of heart; and you shall find rest for your souls. For My yoke is sweet, and My burden light.' We see, then, that God worked six days, and rested on the seventh day. We also must finish our appointed work before we rest: as it is said (Ecclus. li. 35), 'I have laboured a little, and have found much rest for myself.' The difference between a day and a thousand years is as nothing to the difference between this present life and eternity.

4. **For the brightening and strengthening of love.** In the book of Wisdom (ix. 15) we read: 'The corruptible body is a load upon the soul, and the earthly habitation presseth down the mind that museth upon many things.' Man indeed is always sinking down toward earthly things unless he strive to lift himself up

from them; and therefore it is good for him to have fixed times for making this effort.

a. Some spend their whole time in this work: like David (Ps. xxxiii. 2), ' I will bless the Lord at all times; His praise shall be always in my mouth;' or like St. Paul (1 Thess. v. 17), 'Pray without ceasing.' Thus they keep a ceaseless Sabbath.

b. Some do it at fixed intervals. Of them it is said (Ps. cxviii. 164), 'Seven times a day I have given praise to Thee for the judgments of Thy justice.'

c. Others must have an appointed day for this work, lest the love of God should grow cold in them, and they should be utterly alienated from Him. If they have not, they may be drawn away from Him; as Isaias warns us (lviii. 13, 14), ' If thou turn away thy foot from the Sabbath, from doing thy own will in My holy day, and call the Sabbath delightful, and the holy of the Lord glorious, and glorify Him while thou doest not thy own ways, and

thy own will is not found to speak a word,
then shalt thou be delighted in the Lord,
and I will lift thee up above the high
places of the earth, and will feed thee with
the inheritance of Jacob, thy father.' Job
also says (xxii. 26-28), 'Then shalt thou
abound in delights in the Almighty, and
shalt lift up thy face to God. Thou shalt
pray to Him and He will hear thee, and
thou shalt pay thy vows. Thou shalt decree a thing, and it shall come to thee, and
light shall shine in thy ways.' Such days
as these are not ordained for idle play, but
for praising the Lord our God and for praying to Him. St. Augustin therefore says
that it is a less evil on these days to plough
than to play.*

* 'Ludere,' to play, is evidently used here by
St. Augustin and St. Thomas in the scriptural
sense of giving ourselves up to our diversions or
pleasures in such a way as to forget God, neglect-
ing our duty altogether, or at any rate griev-
ously.
'I sat not in the assembly of jesters' (Jerem.
xv. 17).

5. **For acts of kindness to our depen-dants.** Some, being cruel both to them-selves and to their own, work ceaselessly because of the lure of gain. The Jews were very guilty in this way through the greatness of their avarice. Hence there is the command (Deut. v. 12, 14), 'Observe the day of the Sabbath, to sanctify it as the Lord thy God hath commanded thee. . . . Thou shalt not do any work therein, thou, nor thy son, nor thy daughter, nor thy man-servant, nor thy maid-servant, nor thy ox, nor thy ass, nor any of thy beasts, nor the stranger that is within thy gates; that thy man-servant and thy maid-servant may rest,

---

'Never have I joined myself with them that play' (Tobias iii. 17).

'Where are the princes of the nations . . . . that take their diversions with the birds of the air ?' (Baruch iii. 16, 17.)

'The people sat down to eat and drink, and they rose up to play' (Ex. xxxii. 6).

'Neither become ye idolaters, as some of them: as it is written, The people sat down to eat and drink, and rose up to play' (1 Cor. x. 7).

even as thyself.' These, then, are the reasons why this commandment was given.

II. 'Remember to keep holy the Sabbath-day.' It has already been said that, as the Jews keep the Sabbath, we Christians keep the Lord's day and other principal feasts. Let us, then, see how we ought to keep them. In considering this point we must bear in mind that God does not say, Keep holy the Sabbath, but, Remember to keep it holy.

Now the word 'holy' has two meanings. First, it means pure, as when St. Paul says, 'You are washed; you are sanctified,' in a passage of Scripture already quoted. Next, things consecrated to the worship of God are called holy, as, for instance, places, times, vestments, and sacred vessels.

In two ways, therefore, thus signified, we ought to keep the feasts of the Church, that is, not only by purity and cleanness of heart, but also by giving ourselves in a special way to the service of God.

Two things, then, must be considered in this command : (1.) what we ought to avoid on a feast ; and (2.) what we ought to do.

(1.) There are three things from which we should keep ourselves: that is to say, 1. bodily work ; 2. sin ; 3. idleness.

1. **Bodily work.** We read in the law (Lev. xxiii. 3), 'The seventh day, because it is the rest of the Sabbath, shall be called holy. Ye shall do no work on that day.' The work spoken of is servile work. Now servile work is bodily work; but free work is mental work; as, for instance, to understand and the like. With regard to free works a man cannot be bound.

There are, however, four reasons which justify us in doing bodily work on holy days.

a. Necessity. For this reason Jesus excused His disciples when they plucked the ears of corn on the Sabbath. So we read (St. Matt. xii. 1-8), 'At that time Jesus went through the corn on the Sabbath ; and His disciples being hungry began to pluck the corn and to eat. And the Pharisees, seeing them, said to Him, Behold Thy disciples do that which is not lawful to do on the Sabbath-days. But He said to them, Have you not read what David did when he was hungry, and they that were with him? How he entered into the house of God and did eat the loaves of proposition, which it was not lawful for him to eat, nor for them that were with him, but for the priests only? Or have ye not read in the law that on the Sabbath-days the priests in the temple break the Sabbath, and are without blame? But I tell you that there is here a greater than the temple. And if ye knew what this meaneth, I will have mercy, and not sacrifice; ye would never have condemned the innocent. For the Son of man is Lord even of the Sabbath.'

b. The good of the Church. As we have seen in the passage of Scripture last-quoted, our Lord teaches us that the priests could, even on the Sabbath-day, do all things that were needed in the temple.

c. The good of our neighbour. Our Lord healed the man with a withered hand on the Sabbath; and, taking an example from a sheep, silenced the Jews who found fault with Him. All this is written in St. Matthew's Gospel (xii. 10-13), 'Behold there was a man who had a withered hand, and they asked Him, saying, Is it lawful to heal on the Sabbath-days? that they might accuse Him. But He said to them, What man shall there be among you that hath one sheep; and if the same fall into a pit on the Sabbath-day, will he not take hold of it and lift it up? How much better is a man than a sheep? Therefore it is lawful to do a good deed on the Sabbath-days. Then He saith to the man, Stretch forth thy hand; and he stretched it forth; and it was restored to health even as the other.'

d. The authority of a superior. Jesus commanded the Jews to circumcise on the Sabbath, as we learn from St. John (vii. 21): 'Jesus answered and said to them, One work I have done, and ye all wonder. Therefore Moses gave you circumcision ; not because it is of Moses, but of the fathers ; and on the Sabbath-day you circumcise a man. If a man receive circumcision on the Sabbath-day that the law of Moses may not be broken, are you angry at Me, because I have healed the whole man on the Sabbath-day? Judge not according to the appearance, but judge just judgment.'

2. **Sin.** Jeremias says (xvii. 21), 'Thus saith the Lord, Take heed to your souls, and carry no burdens on the Sabbath-day, and bring them not in by the gates of Jerusalem.' Now the burden of the soul, its crushing evil, is sin. Hear the words of David (Ps. xxxvii. 5), 'My iniquities are gone over my head, and as a heavy burden are become heavy upon me.' But sin is a servile work, as Jesus taught (St. John viii. 32-34), 'You shall know the truth, and the truth shall make you free. They answered Him, We are the seed of

Abraham, and we have never been slaves to any man : how sayest Thou, Ye shall be free ? Jesus answered them, Amen, amen, I say to you, that whosoever committeth sin is the servant of sin.' When, therefore, servile work is forbidden, we may well understand it of sin; and thus any one sinning on the Sabbath breaks this commandment, because by working and sinning God is offended. So Isaias teaches (i. 13), 'The new moons and the Sabbaths and other festivals I will not abide.' Why does he speak thus ? He gives the reason : 'because your assemblies are wicked. My soul hateth your new moons and your solemnities; they are become troublesome to me; I am weary of bearing them.'

3. **Idleness.** In Ecclesiasticus it is said (xxxiii. 29), 'Idleness hath taught much evil.' St. Jerome writes thus to Rusticus, 'Always be busied in some good work, that the devil may find you occupied.' But it is useless to be busy in good on the

chief feasts if on other days we give ourselves up to idleness. It is said in the
Psalms (xcviii. 4), 'The king's honour
loveth judgment;' that is to say, loveth
discretion. We read in the first book of
Machabees (ii. 31-38) that certain Jews in
secret places of the wilderness were attacked
by their enemies, and, thinking that they
could not lawfully resist them on the Sabbath, were conquered and slain. So has
it happened to many who give themselves
up to idleness on holy days; as Jeremias
says (Lam. i. 7), 'Her people fell in the
enemy's hand, and there was no helper;
the enemies have seen her and have mocked
at her Sabbaths.' Instead of this we
should do as Mathathias and his friends did
(1 Mac. ii. 41) : 'They determined in that
day, saying, Whosoever shall come up
against us to fight on the Sabbath-day, we
will fight against him; and we will not all
die, as our brethren that were slain in the
secret places.'

'Remember to keep holy the Sabbath-day.' We have seen that we must keep the feasts of the Church holy; and we have also seen that the word 'holy' has two meanings: *a.* that which is pure, and, *b.* that which is consecrated to God. Further, there have been set forth the three things from which we must keep ourselves on such days.

(2.) It remains, then, to speak of the things about which we should be busied.

These things also are three in number.

1. **Sacrifice.** It is said (Ex. xxix. 38, 39), ' This is what thou shalt sacrifice upon the altar: two lambs of a year old, every day continually; one lamb in the morning and another in the evening.' The sacrifice was doubled* on the Sabbath, and so signified that we must offer sacrifice to God, and

* 'On the Sabbath-day you shall offer two lambs of a year old without blemish, and two-tenths of flour tempered with oil in sacrifice; and the libations which regularly are poured out every Sabbath for the perpetual holocaust' (Numb. xxviii. 9, 10).

† ' The king's part was that of his proper sub-

offer it of all that we have. David said
in his prayer and thanksgiving (1 Par.
xxix. 14), 'Who am I, and what is my
people, that we should be able to promise
Thee all these things? All things are
Thine, and we have given Thee what we
have received at Thy hand.' We must
therefore offer three things in sacrifice to
God.

a. Our souls. We do this (*a.*) by griev-
ing over our sins, and (*b.*) by praying for
blessings.

(*a.*) *We grieve over our sins;* according
to the words of the Psalm (l. 19), 'A sacrifice to God is an afflicted spirit; a contrite
and humble heart, O God, Thou wilt not
despise.'

(*b.*) *We pray for blessings* according to
the words of another Psalm (cxl. 1, 2), 'I
have cried to Thee, O Lord, hear me;

---

stance the holocaust should be offered always,
morning and evening, and on the Sabbaths, ...
as it is written in the Law of Moses' (2 Par.
xxxi. 3).

hearken to my voice when I cry to Thee. Let my prayer be offered as incense in Thy sight; and let the lifting up of my hands be as an evening sacrifice.'

Festival days were instituted to fill us with the joy of the Holy Ghost. It is by prayer that we attain this joy, and therefore on such days our prayers ought to be multiplied.

b. Our bodies. We do this (*a.*) by af-flicting them, and (*b.*) by giving praise.

(*a.*) *We afflict our bodies.* This we do, for instance, by fasting;* and of this St. Paul says (Rom. xii. 1), 'I beseech you, therefore, brethren, by the mercy of God, that you present your bodies a living sacri-fice, holy, pleasing unto God, your reason-able service.'

(*b.*) *We give praise.* Of praise the

---

* The Angelic Doctor mentions fasting to com-plete the divisions of his subject, and not as hav-ing anything to do with feasts. He passes it by to speak of our duty of praise; as just before he passed by sorrow to speak of joy.

Psalmist says (xlix. 23), 'The sacrifice of praise shall glorify Me, and there is the way by which I will show him the salvation of God.'

On festival days, then, like these, songs of praise should be multiplied.

c. Our goods. We should give alms. Here is the command (Heb. xiii. 16), 'To do good and to impart forget not; for by such sacrifices God's favour is obtained.' Now, because of the common joy, there is a twofold reason for giving on festivals. Hence it was said to all the people by Nehemias and Esdras (2 Esdr. viii. 10), 'Go eat fat meats and drink sweet wine, and send portions to them that have not prepared for themselves, because it is the holy day of the Lord; and be not sad, for the joy of the Lord is our strength.'

2. The study of God's word. This was the custom of the Jews in the time of our Lord (Acts xiii. 27): 'They that inhabited Jerusalem, and the rulers thereof, not knowing Him, nor the voices of the prophets, which are read every Sabbath, judging Him have fulfilled them.' Christians, therefore, whose holiness ought to be greater than theirs, should on these days, *a.* meet together for two things ; and, *b.* should engage in profitable conversation.

a. They should meet together (a.) to listen to sermons, and (b.) to take part in the offices of the Church. Our Lord says (St. John viii. 47), 'He that is of God heareth the words of God.'

b. They should also speak of things that are profitable for good : according to St. Paul's teaching (Eph. iv. 29), 'Let no evil speech proceed from your mouth, but that which is good for the edification of faith, that it may minister grace to the hearers.' Very useful are both of these practices to the sinful soul, for by them the heart is changed and led on to holiness. Hear the words of Jeremias (xxiii. 29) : 'Are not My words as a fire, saith the Lord, and as a hammer that breaketh the rock in pieces ?'

K

On the other hand, there must be a
change for the worse in the imperfect, who
neither speak words that are good for others,
nor listen to words that are good for themselves. St. Paul warns us (1 Cor. xv.
33, 34), 'Be not deceived. Evil commu-
nications corrupt good manners. Awake,
ye just, and sin not. For some have not
the knowledge of God ; I speak it to your
shame.' Job also says (xxiii. 12), 'The
words of His mouth I have hidden in my
bosom ;' and the Psalmist (cxviii. 11),
'Thy words have I hidden in my heart, that
I may not sin against Thee.' The word of
God enlightens the dark soul and kindles
the cold soul ; as it is said (Ps. cxviii. 105),
'Thy word is a lamp to my feet, and a light
to my paths ;' and again, as before (Ps.
civ. 19), 'The word of the Lord inflamed
him.'

3. **Spiritual Exercises.** This, however,
is the work of the perfect. We read (Ps.
xlv. 11), 'Be still, and see that I am God ;'
and again (Ps. xxxiii. 9), 'O taste and see

that the Lord is sweet.' These things are written that the soul may find rest; for as a wearied body longs for rest, so longeth also a wearied soul. But the only resting-place of the soul is God. Therefore it is written (Heb. iv. 8-11), 'If Jesus had given them rest, He would not afterwards have spoken of another day. There remaineth therefore a day of rest for the people of God. For he that hath entered into his rest hath rested from his works, as God did from His. Let us hasten therefore to enter into that rest.'

Before the soul can reach this rest it must have attained tranquillity in three ways.

a. From the disquiet of sin. There are the words of Isaias (lvii. 20, 21), 'The wicked are like the raging sea which cannot rest; and the waves thereof cast up dirt and mire. There is no peace to the wicked, saith the Lord God.'

b. From the disquiet of fleshly passions. The Apostle tells us this (Gal. v. 17-25),

' The flesh lusteth against the spirit, and the spirit against the flesh : for these are contrary one to another, so that you do not the things that you would. But if you are led by the Spirit you are not under the law. Now the works of the flesh are manifest, which are fornication, uncleanness, immodesty, luxury, idolatry, witchcrafts, enmities, contentions, emulations, wraths, quarrels, dissensions, sects, envies, murders, drunkenness, revellings, and such-like : of which I forewarn you, as I have forewarned you that they who do such things shall not attain the kingdom of God. But the fruit of the Spirit is love, joy, peace, patience, kindness, goodness, long-suffering, mildness, faith, modesty, continence, chastity. Against such there is no law : and they that are Christ's have crucified the flesh with its vices and desires. If we live in the Spirit let us also walk in the Spirit.'

c. From the disquiet of worldly occupations. Jesus said to Martha (St. Luke x. 41, 42), ' Martha, Martha, thou art careful and art troubled about many things. But one thing is necessary. Mary hath chosen the best part, which shall not be taken away from her.'

After these three quiets are gained, the soul freely rests in God, as we have seen before. Isaias says (lviii. 13, 14), 'If thou .... call the Sabbath delightful, and the holy of the Lord glorious, ... then shalt thou be delighted in the Lord.' Moreover the saints have cast away everything to gain this peace. It is the pearl of great price of which Jesus speaks (St. Matt. xiii. 45, 46): 'The kingdom of heaven is like to a merchant seeking good pearls, who when he had found one pearl of great price went his way, and sold all that he had, and bought it.' It is also the hidden treasure (v. 44): 'The kingdom of heaven is like a treasure hidden in a field, which a man having found hid, and for joy thereof goeth and selleth all that he hath and buyeth that field.' This rest, indeed, is the everlasting life and the everlasting joy. Of this the

Psalmist speaks when he says (cxxxi. 14),
'This is my rest for ever and ever: here
will I dwell, for I have chosen it.' May
God bring us to the blessedness of the rest
that never ends.

Prayer.

In six days Thou didst make all things,
O ever-blessed Trinity, and on the seventh
day didst rest from the works that Thou
hadst made. Yet dost Thou work always
in sustaining Thy creation. Jesus said,
'My Father worketh hitherto, and I work.'

By the first man we are of the earth
earthy; but by the second Man we are of
heaven. Adam died, and Jesus liveth for
evermore. Whereas Israel kept Thy day
because of the works of creation, we keep
it for the light of Thy new creation, and
for the rising of Jesus from the dead. St.
John was in the Spirit on the Lord's day.

O God of peace, Thou givest rest to Thy
people. We wait longingly for our threefold rest: our rest from work and toil: our

rest from the fiery bitterness of temptations: our rest from the iron slavery of the devil and sin.

Thou givest us rest even here in the sweet yoke of Jesus and the lightness of His burden. Thou kindlest our love and givest us wisdom, that we may know how to look onward to the eternal rest that remaineth for Thy people, and how to desire it.

We pray for grace to keep ourselves from servile work, from idleness, from the guilt of sin. May we always be in our places at the very beginning of the adorable Sacrifice of the Mass; and may our prayers be multiplied before Thee. Let us take great delight in being much in Thy house on Thy holy days. Let us not forget to give alms in honour of Thee and according to Thy will. O may we always find great delight in Thy sacred Scriptures, the word of life, more precious than gold. May we always know and understand our own ignorance and our need of instruction. So may we listen with reverence to the words of Thy preachers. Thy word, O my God, is a kindled brightness and a flaming fire.

Give me rest, my loving God, from the cares of the world, from fleshly passions, from the restlessness of sin. Let this be to me a prelude of the wealthy rest in heaven. Lead me, by the sweetness of Thy hand, from the tabernacles of confidence to the beauty of the unending peace. There is the resting-place of the soul, O adorable Trinity, Father, Son, and Holy Ghost, where it resteth evermore in Thee.

CHAPTER IX.

OF THE FOURTH COMMANDMENT OF THE LAW.

I. 'HONOUR thy father and thy mother, that thou mayest be long-lived in the land which the Lord thy God will give thee' (Ex. xx. 12).

The perfection of man consists in the love of God and the love of his neighbour.

To the love of God pertain the three commandments which were written on the first table ; and to the love of our neighbour pertain the other seven, which were written on the second table.

But, as we have seen, we ought to love not only in word and in tongue, but in deed and in truth. Man, therefore, loving in this way, ought to do two things, that is to say, he ought to fly from what is evil and cleave to what is good. Some of the commandments, therefore, lead us to good, while others keep us back from evil.

We must bear in mind, however, that it is in our power to keep from evil, whereas it is not always in our power to do good to others. For this reason Blessed Augustin said that we are bound to love all men, but we are not bound to do acts of kindness to all.* Most of all ought we to do acts of kindness to our kindred, according

* We cannot have the time or the means for such works ; and so they are out of our power, however much we may wish to do them.

to St. Paul's teaching (1 Tim. v. 8), 'If any man have not care of his own, and especially of those of his house, he hath denied the faith, and is worse than an infidel.' But father and mother are the nearest to us of all our relatives; and therefore St. Ambrose says that, loving God first, we should next love our father and mother; and that this is why God says, 'Honour thy father and thy mother.'

The Philosopher gives a natural reason for this duty to parents, saying, that we can never make them an adequate return for what they have done, so great are the benefits which we have received from them; and that therefore a father being angry has a right to send away his son from his house, while a son has no such right with regard to his father. Now children have three gifts from their parents.

1. **Their existence.** Thus it is said (Ecclus. vii. 29, 30), 'Honour thy father, and forget not the groanings of thy mother. Remember that thou hadst not been born

but through them ; and make a return to them as they have done for thee.'

2. **Nourishment or support with regard to the necessaries of life.** It is said in the Book of Job (i. 21), 'Naked came I out of my mother's womb, and naked shall I return thither.' Children, having nothing, are kept and supported by their parents.

3. **Instruction.** So the Apostle says (Heb. xii. 9, 10), 'We have had fathers of our flesh for instructors, and we reverenced them ; shall we not much more obey the Father of spirits, and live? They indeed for a few days, according to their own pleasure, instructed us ; but He for our profit, that we might receive His sanctification.' Again (Ecclus. vii. 25), 'Hast thou children? Instruct them.' The instruction that parents ought to give to their children is twofold : *a.* to fear God, and, *b.* to keep from sin. This instruction ought to be given promptly, for first we read (Prov. xxii. 6), 'It is a proverb: A young man

according to his way, and even when he is old he will not depart from it;' and next (Lam. iii. 27), 'It is good for a man when he hath borne the yoke from his youth.'

Such was the instruction which Tobias gave to his son (Tobias i. 10): 'From his infancy he taught him to fear God, and to abstain from all sin.'

These words are spoken against parents who take pleasure in the wickedness of their children. In Ecclesiasticus it is said (iv. 6), 'The children that are borne of unlawful beds are witnesses of wickedness against their parents at their trial.' Thus God punishes in the children the sin of the parents.

II. We see, then, that from their parents children receive, 1. existence, 2. support, 3. instruction; and it follows that each of these things lays on us a duty to our father and mother.

1. **Reverence.** Because we receive our being from them we should reverence them more than all our masters but God. From

masters we receive only material gifts, but God gives us our souls.   It is said (Ecclus. iii. 8-10), 'He that feareth the Lord honoureth his parents, and will serve them as his masters that brought him into the world. Honour thy father in work and word and all patience, that a blessing may come upon thee from him, and that his blessing may remain in the latter end.' We must honour our fathers and our mothers that a blessing may come on us from God.   In doing this we honour ourselves ; as it is said (Ecclus. iii. 12), 'The glory of a man is from the honour of his father, and a father without honour is the disgrace of his son.'

2. **Succour.** Because we receive support from them in our childhood we ought to succour them in their old age.   This we are taught (Ecclus. iii. 14, 15), 'Son, support the old age of thy father, and grieve him not in his life ; and if his understanding fail have patience with him, and despise him not when thou art in thy strength ; for the relieving of the father shall not be

forgotten.' So again (v. 18), 'Of what an evil fame is he that forsaketh his father; and he is cursed of God that angereth his mother.'

To the shame of those who neglect and dishonour their parents, Cassiodorus, in one of his letters, tells us about the cranes. When they lose their feathers in old age, and cannot find fit food for themselves, their young ones warm them and feed them, giving back to their parents in a kindly return of care the help that they themselves received when young.

3. **Obedience.** Because we receive instruction from them, we must give them obedience. St. Paul says (Col. iii. 20), 'Children, obey your parents in all things; for this is well-pleasing to the Lord.' That means, of course, in all things that are not against the will of God. If they command us to do what is contrary to God's law, then, as St. Jerome writes, 'The only true filial piety in such a case is to be cruel.' For our Lord says, as we have seen before (St.

Luke xiv. 26), 'If any man come to Me, and hate not his father, and mother, and wife, and children, and brethren, and sisters, yea, and his own life also, he cannot be My disciple.'   He speaks thus, because God is most truly our father.   Again, it is said (Deut. xxxii. 6), 'Is this the return thou makest to the Lord, O foolish and senseless people?   Is not He thy Father that hath possessed thee, and made thee, and created thee?'   Again (v. 18.), 'Thou hast forsaken the God that begot thee, and hast forgotten the Lord that created thee.' Isaias also says (lxiii. 16), 'Thou art our Father, and Abraham hath not known us and Israel hath been ignorant of us.   Thou, O Lord, art our Father, our Redeemer; from everlasting is Thy name.'

III. 'Honour thy father and thy mother, that thou mayest be long-lived in the land which the Lord thy God will give thee.' This is the only commandment, for keeping which long life here is promised as a reward.   The reason is plain: it is lest any

one should think that a reward is not due
to those who honour their parents, because
such honour is according to the dictates of
nature. We should moreover understand
that five desirable things are here promised
to the honourers of father and mother.

1. **Grace here and the promise of glory
hereafter.** Grace and glory are to be desired above all other things. It is said
(Ecclus. iii. 9, 10), 'Honour thy father in
work and word and all patience, that a
blessing may come upon thee from him, and
that his blessing may remain in the latter
end.' Honour thy father that a blessing
may come on thee from God.

On the other hand a curse is due to
those who curse their parents, and even in
the law they are cursed by God. Our
Lord said (St. Luke xvi. 10), ' He that is
unjust in that which is little, is unjust also
in that which is greater.' Now the life of
nature is as nothing to the life of grace. If,
then, thou understandest not the blessings
of the natural life which thou hast from

thy father and thy mother, thou dost not deserve to have the life of grace, which is greater, and still less dost thou deserve the life of glory, which is greater still.

2. **Life.** Long life is promised to them; as it is said (Ecclus. iii. 7), ' He that honoureth his father shall enjoy a long life.'

Here you must bear in mind that a long life is a full life; and that the fulness of life is measured by action and not by time. Indeed a life is full when it is virtuous; and therefore a holy man, living virtuously, lives long, even though he be cut off by death quickly. Hence it is said in Wisdom (iv. 13, 14), ' Being made perfect in a short space, he fulfilled a long time; for his soul pleased God. Therefore He hastened to bring him out of the midst of iniquities. But the people see this, and understand not, nor lay up such things in their hearts.' He indeed works well who does in one day what another does in a year.

Besides we should remember that sometimes the lengthening of a life is the cause

L

of bodily death and of spiritual death.*
So it was with Judas. The reward, then,
is bodily life, but they who injure their
parents are punished with death. We
hold our lives from our parents, as soldiers
hold their fiefs from the king. As then
they justly lose their fiefs for treason, so
we justly lose our lives for injuries inflicted
on our parents ; as it is said (Prov. xxx.
17), 'The eye that mocketh at his father
and that despiseth the labour of his mother
in bearing him, let the ravens of the brooks
pick it out, and let the young eagles eat it.'
By the young eagles are understood kings
and rulers. By the ravens are understood
their ministers. If the dishonourers of
parents are not always punished with bodily
death, yet they cannot escape the death
of the soul.

* St. Thomas means that if the life of Judas
had been shortened, he would not have come to
so fearful a death as that by which he died.
Not only did he die spiritually as to his soul,
but also by a violent and shameful death as to
his body.

Moreover, a father ought not to give too much power to his sons (Ecclus. xxxiii. 20, 21): ' Give not to son or wife, brother or friend, power over thee while thou livest; and give not thy estate to another, lest thou repent and thou entreat for the same. As long as thou livest, and hast breath in thee, let no man change thee.'

3. **Good children.** They themselves will have kind and grateful children. Naturally the father lays up for the son, and not the son for the father. St. Paul says of himself (2 Cor. xii. 14), ' I seek not the things that are yours, but you. For the children ought not to lay up for the parents, but the parents for the children.' It is said therefore (Ecclus. iii. 6), ' He that honoureth his father shall have joy in his own children.' Our Lord also says (St. Matt. vii. 2), ' With what measure you mete it shall be measured to you again.'

4. **A good report.** They will have an honourable report among men. As was said before, ' The glory of a man is from

the honour of his father.' Again (Ecclus. iii. 18), 'Of what an evil fame is he that forsaketh his father; and he is cursed of God that angereth his mother.'

5. **Prosperity.** They will have riches. It is said (Ecclus. iii. 11), 'The father's blessing establisheth the houses of the children; but the mother's curse rooteth up the foundations.'

IV. 'Honour thy father.' There is another point to be considered. We do not only call men fathers because of carnal birth, but we give them that name for five other reasons. According to each of these reasons we owe them a due honour.

1. **The Apostles.** The Apostles and other Saints are called fathers because of their teaching and the example of faith. St. Paul says to the Corinthians (1 Ep. iv. 15), 'If you have ten thousand instructors in Christ, yet not many fathers. For in Christ Jesus I have begotten you by the Gospel.' In like manner it is said (Ecclus. xliv. 1), 'Let us now praise men of re-

nown and our fathers in their generation.'
We have not, however, to praise them only
with our lips, but by imitation of their
lives. Now this is done if there be found
nothing in us unlike that which we praise.
So it is said (Heb. xiii. 7, 8), 'Remember
your prelates who have spoken the word
of God to you; whose faith follow, considering the end of their conversation,
Jesus Christ, the same yesterday and to-
day and for ever.'

2. **Prelates.** They who are set over us
spiritually are our fathers, and they have to
be reverenced because they are ministers of
God; according to the saying of our Lord
(St. Luke x. 16), 'He that heareth you,
heareth Me; and he that despiseth you,
despiseth Me; and he that despiseth Me,
despiseth Him that sent Me.'

We must, therefore, show our reverence
for the ministers of God in two ways:
a. by obeying them; and, *b.* by contributing
to their support.

a, Obedience. We must be obedient to

them (Heb. xiii. 17), 'Obey your prelates, and be subject to them. For they watch, as having to render an account of your souls, that they may do this with joy, and not with grief.'

b. Support. We must pay them tithes* (Prov. iii. 9, 10): 'Honour the Lord with thy substance, and give Him the first of all thy fruits; and thy barns shall be filled with abundance, and thy presses shall run over with wine.'

3. **Rulers.** Kings and rulers are also called our fathers. Thus (4 Kings v. 13), 'His servants came to him' (Naaman) 'and said to him, Father, if the prophet had bidden thee do some great thing, surely thou shouldest have done it? How much rather what he now hath said to thee, Wash, and thou shalt be clean.' They are called fathers because they are bound to seek earnestly for the good of their people. We honour them by subjection; as St. Paul

* That is to say, we must contribute to their support.

says (Rom. xiii. 1, 2), 'Let every soul be
subject to higher powers; for there is no
power but from God; and those that are,
are ordained of God. Therefore he that
resisteth the power resisteth the ordinance
of God.' We give them this reverence, not
only through fear but through love; not
only by reason but also by conscience. We
do so because of the teaching of the Apostle,
who says that all power is from God; and
who also says (v. 7), 'Render therefore to
all men their dues: tribute to whom tribute
is due; custom, to whom custom; fear, to
whom fear; honour, to whom honour.' It
is therefore said (Prov. xxiv. 21), 'My son,
fear the Lord and the king.'

4. **Benefactors.** Benefactors are called
our fathers. The Scripture says (Ecclus.
iv. 10), 'In judging be merciful to the
fatherless as a father:' for this is the cha-
racteristic of a father. Again (Ecclus. xxix.
19), 'Forget not the kindness of thy surety;'
for that is what the thankless do. Of them
it is said (Wisd. xvi. 29), 'The hope of the

unthankful shall melt away as the winter's ice, and shall run off as unprofitable water.'

5. **Age.** The old are called our fathers. Thus we read (Deut. xxxii. 7), 'Ask thy father, and he will declare to thee; thy elders, and they will tell thee.' Again (Lev. xix. 32), 'Rise up before the hoary head, and honour the person of the aged man, and fear the Lord thy God. I am the Lord.' Again (Ecclus. xxxii. 13), 'In the company of great men take not upon thee; and when the ancients are present speak not much.' So again (v. 9), 'Hear in silence, and for thy reverence good grace shall come to thee.'

All such persons, therefore, are to be reverenced, because they all bear in different ways the likeness of our Father who is in heaven. To them we may apply the words, 'He who despiseth you, despiseth Me.'

Prayer.

O adorable Trinity, One God, Thou art Lord of all and Father of all. To Thee all creatures do homage, and in Thee they live. Thou art my Father, and I give honour to Thee, in the highest and for Thy own sake. Whatever honour I give to other fathers, I give for Thy sake and in Thee.

From our earthly father and mother we receive our bodies and nourishment and instruction, but far more do we receive these gifts from Thee, our Maker and Keeper. As we owe our father and mother reverence and help and obedience for these blessings, so far more do we owe all reverence and all obedience to Thee, who art infinitely above all need of help, being almighty and all-wise.

Give me grace, O God, to follow in the steps of Jesus. As He loved His heavenly Father and His earthly mother, so give me much love for my father and mother. (Here pray for them, and for all their needs on earth or in Purgatory.) May I always show them love, reverence, honour, and obedience according to Thy will. May I always give them all the help I can here;

and may I always give them all the help that they need in Purgatory.

O adorable Trinity, let my life be a full life in Thee, that it may be a long life in virtue, however short a life it may be in days. If it be Thy holy will that it should be a long life in days, let it be far longer in holiness and in love of Thee.

O my God, may I have great reverence for the Vicar of Jesus Christ, the Saviour whom I love; and may I have great reverence for all bishops and priests who stand at Thy altars and serve Thee.

For Thy sake, O God, I submit myself to rulers and teachers, and those who are in any way set over me lawfully.

May I never forget my benefactors, but always remember them with gratitude, and always do what I can for them in return.

May I always be full of respect for the aged; remembering that a hoary head found in the way of holiness is as a crown of justice; and that Thou hast told me to rise up and honour the person of the aged man, and fear Thee, the Lord my God.

O God, Thou art my Father, may I always live as Thy child, reverencing Thee only for Thyself, and submitting myself to all authorities in Thee and for Thee.

O adorable Trinity, Thou art my dearest Father and my own God.

CHAPTER X.

OF THE FIFTH COMMANDMENT OF THE LAW.

'Thou shalt not kill' (Ex. xx. 13). By the divine law which sets charity in order in us, with regard to the love of God and our neighbour, we are commanded not only to do right, but also to keep from wrong. Now the greatest evil that we can bring on our neighbour is death. We have therefore the command, 'Thou shalt not kill.'

I. Men have erred about this commandment in three ways.

1. **As to animals.** Some have said that
it is not lawful to kill brute animals. This
is false ; for there can be no sin in our using
animals when they have been put under
the power of man. Indeed there is a natural order by which plants are for the nourishment of animals; certain animals for
the nourishment of one another; and all
for the nourishment of man. So God said
to Noe and his sons (Gen. ix. 3), 'Every
thing that moveth and liveth shall be meat
for you; even as the green herbs have I
delivered them all to you.' The Philosopher says in his Politics that hunting* is
like a just war. St. Paul also says (1 Cor.
x. 25, 26), 'Whatsoever is sold in the
shambles, eat; asking no questions for conscience' sake. The earth is the Lord's, and
the fulness thereof.' The command therefore means thou shalt not kill men.

2. **Punishment of death.** Some have

---

* That is, hunting for the sake of food, or for
the destruction of noxious animals which cannot
otherwise be destroyed.

said that by this command it is forbidden to kill a man in any way whatever. As a consequence, they have taught that judges who condemn men to death by the law are murderers. St. Augustin answers them, saying that God did not take away from Himself the power of life and death by this command; for He says (Deut. xxxii. 39), 'I will kill and I will make to live.' It is .lawful, therefore, to slay when the slaying is by the command of God; for then it is God who does it, every law being a command of God. Thus God says (Prov. viii. 14-16), 'Counsel and equity are mine, prudence is mine, strength is mine. By Me kings reign and lawgivers decree just things. By Me princes rule and the mighty decree justice.' St. Paul also says (Rom. xiii. 4), 'If thou do that which is evil, fear; for he beareth not the sword in vain. For he is God's minister: an avenger to execute wrath upon him that doeth evil.' An express command was given by God to Moses (Ex. xxii. 18): 'Wizards thou shalt

not suffer to live.' Again (v. 20), 'He
that sacrificeth to gods, save only to the
Lord, shall be put to death.' What, therefore, is lawful for God Himself is lawful
for God's ministers, by God's command.
Now since God is the maker of the law, it
is plain that He does not sin when, because of sin, He inflicts the punishment of
death; for as St. Paul says (Rom. vi. 23),
'The wages of sin is death.' Therefore it
follows that God's ministers do not sin in
like cases. The meaning of the commandment, then, is, Thou shalt not kill on thy
own authority.

3. **Suicide.** Some again have said that
the being forbidden to kill others shows
that it is lawful for a man to kill himself.
They give such instances as Samson and
Cato and certain virgins, who threw themselves into the fire, as St. Augustin mentions in the first book of the *City of God.*
But St. Augustin gives the answer in the
same place: 'He who kills himself certainly kills a human being; but if it be

only lawful to kill a human being by the authority of God, it is only lawful to kill one's self by the authority of God or the inspiration of the Holy Ghost, as indeed Samson did.'

II. Further, there are many ways of killing.

1. **By the hand.** It is said (Isaias i. 15), 'When you stretch forth your hands, I will turn away My eyes from you; and when you multiply prayer, I will not hear; for your hands are full of blood.' Murder, indeed, is not only, *a.* against charity, which commands us to love our neighbour as ourselves, but also, *b.* against nature.

a. Of one St. John says (1 Ep. iii. 15), 'Whosoever hateth his brother is a murderer; and you know that no murderer hath eternal life abiding in him.'

b. Of the other it is said (Ecclus. xiii. 19), 'Every beast loveth its like.' Hence the command of Moses (Ex. xxi. 12), 'He that striketh a man with a will to kill him shall be put to death.'

A murderer is more cruel than a wolf, of whom some one has said that he will not eat the flesh of another wolf.

2. **By mouth.** We do this if we excite one person against another, by provoking or accusing or detracting. It is said in the Psalms (lvi. 5), 'The sons of men, whose teeth are weapons and arrows, and their tongue a sharp sword.'

3. **By help.** So it is said (Prov. i. 15, 16), 'My son, walk not thou with them: restrain thy foot from their paths. For their feet run to evil, and make haste to shed blood.'

4. **By consent.** St. Paul says (Rom. i. 32), 'Who, having known the justice of God, did not understand that they who do such things are worthy of death; and not only they that do them, but they also that consent to them that do them.' We can consent in two ways: *a.* when we can hinder, and do not; or, *b.* when we have power to help, and fail through carelessness or avarice.

a. Hence it is said in Proverbs (xxiv. 11, 12), 'Deliver them that are led to death; and those that are drawn to death forbear not to deliver. If thou say, I have not strength enough, He that seeth into the heart understandeth, and nothing de-ceiveth the keeper of thy soul; and He shall render to a man according to his works.'

b. St. Ambrose also says, 'Feed the man who is dying of hunger. If thou feedest him not, thou killest him.'

As to the soul. We must bear carefully in mind that, whereas, as we have seen, some kill only the body, others kill the soul by depriving it of the life of grace. They do this by leading it into mortal sin. Our Lord said of the devil (St. John viii. 44), 'He was a murderer from the begin-ning,' because he led man into sin.

*Both body and soul.** There are some

---

* St. Thomas, as we see from his own words in this note, does not mean that the souls of chil-dren dying unborn are killed in the sense in

M

who do both, and that in two ways: (*a*.) by
the destruction of mother and child, and
(*b*.) by the destruction of themselves.

------

which a soul in mortal sin is killed; but that,
though they will have a natural happiness, they
are incapable of possessing the vision of God.

The following doctrine about the punishment
of original sin is taken from Suarez, ad 1^m 2^{ae}
St. Thom. Tr. 5, Disp. 9, sect. 6 :

1. It is of faith that souls leaving this life in
original sin only cannot see God.

2. St. Thomas (2, dist. 33, q. 12, a. 2), St. Bonaventure (2 p. dist., q. 2), Richard (4, dist. 50,
q. ult.), and Suarez himself teach that, according
to the truer opinion, this does not cause them
pain.

3. They will not suffer any pain of sense. This
also is taught by St. Thomas, St. Bonaventure,
and Richard. St. Thomas (q. 5, de Malo, a. 2)
says that pain of sense is inflicted for turning to
evil, which these children did not do.

4. Suarez goes on to say, 'After the resurrection the state of their souls will be the same
as before ; but in body they will only suffer the
loss of the glory which pertains to the body. So
teach St. Thomas and all, as above. Hence I infer
that those children will have a true natural
knowledge of God, and a love of Him above all

III. 'Thou shalt not kill.' Our Lord says in the Gospel (St. Matt. v. 20), 'I tell you that, unless your justice abound

---

things. They will also have the other natural virtues, and bodies incapable of suffering pain. . . They will not need food or drink. . . They will not suffer any rebellion of the appetites nor any warfare, either inward or outward. Almost all theologians agree as to these points ; though some think that they will be in a gloomy place ; while others think with piety and probability that their dwelling-place will be in this world.'

'(These) children . . . . were never made capable (proportionati) of possessing eternal life, and so they suffer nothing whatever through want of the vision of God. Nay, rather they rejoice in this—that they have a great share of the goodness of God and of natural perfections.' *St. Thom. Supplem.* q. 71, a. 2, *alias Appendicis*, q. 1, a. 2.

'Though unbaptised children are separated from God, so far as regards the union with Him by glory, yet they are not altogether separated from Him. Rather are they joined to Him by a participation of natural goods ; and therefore they will be able to rejoice about Him by natural knowledge and love.' *St. Thom. Ibid.* a. 5.

We must bear in mind ' that these children are

more than that of the Scribes and Pharisees, you shall not enter into the kingdom
of heaven.' Our justice must be greater
than the justice of the law,—that is to say,
we Christians must keep the commandments more perfectly than the Jews kept
them. The reason for this is that it needs
greater toil to gain a greater reward; as
the Apostle teaches (2 Cor. ix. 6), 'Now
this I say, He who soweth sparingly shall
reap also sparingly; and he who soweth

---

not properly called "blessed" (beatos), though
they have this natural happiness, which answers
perfectly to a state of pure nature.' Schouppe,
vol. ii., Tr. xix. 85.

Thus St. Thomas and others teach. Still we
can see how grievous a sin it must be to do
anything which may bring about so great a
loss to a soul as the loss of the vision of God.
Whatever natural happiness a soul may have, we
kill it in a true sense if we deprive it for ever
of the Beatific Vision. All natural bliss is as
nothing compared with the intuitive vision of
the Adorable Trinity, Father, Son, and Holy
Ghost, the One God.

in blessings shall also reap of blessings.'
In the old law they were promised temporal and earthly rewards. Isaias says (i.
19), 'If you be willing and will hearken
to Me, you shall eat the good things of the
land.' But in our law we are promised rewards that are heavenly and everlasting.
Therefore justice, which is the keeping of
the commandments, ought to abound according to the greatness of the reward for
which we look. Now, among other commands, our Lord speaks of this, saying
(St. Matt. v. 21, 22), 'You have heard
that it was said to them of old, Thou shalt
not kill; and whosoever shall kill shall
be in danger of the judgment. But I say
to you that whosoever is angry with his
brother shall be in danger of the judgment.' He alludes to the punishment
fixed by the law, where it is said (Ex. xxi.
14), 'If a man kill his neighbour on set
purpose and by lying in wait for him,
thou shalt take him away from My Altar
that he may die.'

There are five ways in which we ought to be on our guard against anger.

(1.) **Provocation.** We must take care not to be easily provoked. St. James says (i. 19, 20), 'Let every man be swift to hear, but slow to speak and slow to anger. For the anger of man worketh not the justice of God.' There are two reasons for these words; that is, 1. Sin, and 2. Slavery.

1. **Sin.** Anger is a sin, therefore we are punished for it by God. Here, however, we must inquire whether all anger is contrary to virtue. As to this, philosophers have held two opinions.

The Stoics said that no passion touches a wise man. Nay more, they taught that true virtue is to be found in tranquillity of mind.

On the other hand, the Peripatetics said that a wise man may rightly be angry, but with moderation. This is the truer opinion, and its truth is evident in two ways; *a*, by authority, and, *b*, by reason.

a. By authority. In the Gospel we find

such passions* attributed to our Lord; and we know that in Him was the fontal fulness of wisdom.

b. By reason. If all passions were contrary to virtue, there would be some powers of the soul which would be useless; nay, further, which would be actually hurtful to man, because they could not be developed in any fitting acts. Thus the irascible faculties and the concupiscible

---

* Suarez teaches that there were in our Lord 'affections which are called passions in us;' but that He did not have them 'with the imperfections which are found in us, and which are contrary to a perfect state of holiness.' Further, they are simply called passions, as it seems, by St. Thomas and St. Cyril; as also by St. Ambrose, St. John of Damascus, and the 6th Synod. 'This without any doubt is true, and we may safely speak thus among those who understand.' But yet, because the word is often taken in a bad sense, to signify something inordinate and unbridled, St. Jerome prefers the word ' propassions.' Suarez adds: 'This way of speaking commends itself to us because of the great reverence due to Christ.' (Suarez, Disp. xxxiv. in 3. St. Thomæ, Sect. i. 5).

faculties would have been given to man uselessly and without any purpose. We must conclude, therefore, that anger sometimes is a sin and sometimes is not. To understand this we must bear in mind that anger may be looked at in three ways.

(*a.*) *In the reason.* Anger may be wholly according to the judgment of reason, without any disturbance of the mind; that, however, is not rightly called anger, but judgment. In this way, God Himself, punishing the wicked, is said to be angry. The prophet Micheas says (vii. 9), 'I will bear the wrath of the Lord, because I have sinned against Him, until He judge my cause and execute judgment for me. He will bring me forth into the light; I will behold His justice.'

Next, anger may be taken as a passion existing in the sensitive appetite. But, looked at thus, anger is (*b.*) sometimes according to reason and (*c.*) sometimes not. (These two cases therefore make up the three just mentioned.)

(b.) *In the sensitive appetite, reasonably.*
Anger, in the sensitive appetite, may be
ordered by reason and kept within the
bounds of reason. Thus a man may be
angry when he ought to be, and so much
as he ought to be, and with whom he ought
to be, and so on. Then it is an act of virtue, and is called the anger of zeal. Hence
the Philosopher says that meekness is not
the being without anger, under any circumstances whatever. When we are justly
and rightly angry it is not a sin.

(c.) *In the sensitive appetite, unreason-
ably.* Anger in the sensitive appetite may
throw off all restraints of reason and right
judgment. That is always a sin; sometimes venial, sometimes mortal. The dis-
tinction has to be sought from that which
leads us to anger, for that motive may be
a mortal sin. Now a sin is mortal in two
ways, either in its own nature or from the
circumstances. But murder seems to be
an act of mortal sin in its own nature, because it goes right against the command of

God. Therefore consent to murder is a mortal sin in its own nature; for if the act be mortal sin, the consent to the act is mortal sin also. Sometimes, however, a sin may be mortal in its own nature, and yet the movement in the soul towards it may not be a mortal sin, inasmuch as it is without full consent. So you may be tempted by wrong desire to a sin of impurity, and yet keep from mortal sin by not giving consent. The same thing also must be said with regard to anger. There comes, for instance, a movement of soul to avenge an injury that has been done, for this properly is anger. If the movement be of such a nature that reason is utterly put aside, the sin is mortal. If reason be not perverted to full consent, the sin is venial. But if the movement be not in its own nature a mortal sin, then, though consent be given, the sin is not mortal. When, then, our Lord says, 'Whosoever is angry with his brother shall be in danger of the judgment,' we must understand Him to speak of a movement tending to great injury, that movement being a mortal sin, because there is consent enough. Scripture, therefore, says (Eccles. xii. 14), 'All things that are done God will bring to judgment for every error, whether it be good or evil.'

2. **Slavery.** The second reason why we should be slow to anger is because every one loves freedom and hates slavery. For an angry man is not master of himself; as it is said (Prov. xxvii. 3, 4), 'A stone is heavy and sand weighty; but the anger of a fool is heavier than them both. Anger hath no mercy, nor hath fury, when it breaketh forth; and who can bear the fury of one provoked?'

(2.) **Continuance in anger.** We should guard against continuing in anger. The Psalmist says (iv. 5), 'Be ye angry and sin not;' and St. Paul (Eph. iv. 26), 'Be angry and sin not. Let not the sun go down upon your anger.' Our Lord gives the reason for this in the Gospel (St. Matt.

v. 25, 26), 'Be at agreement with thy adversary betimes while thou art in the way with him, lest perhaps the adversary deliver thee to the judge and the judge deliver thee to the officer, and thou be cast into prison. Amen, I say to thee, thou shalt not go out from thence till thou repay the last farthing.'

(3.) **Growth of anger.** We should guard against the growth of anger. This point has to be considered in three ways,* that is, with regard to our hearts and lips and works.

1. *As to the heart.* Anger growing in the heart comes to hatred ; for there is a difference between anger and hatred. Anger is sudden, but hatred is lasting. Now hatred is a mortal sin ; as St. John says (1 Ep. iii. 15), 'Whosoever hateth his brother is a murderer.' The reason of this is that he not only slays another, but slays himself also, by stripping himself of charity. St. Augustin says in his rule, 'Have no quarrels among yourselves, or at any rate

* Making up the five points mentioned, p. 166.

end them as soon as you can, lest anger should grow into hatred, making a beam out of a mote, and filling the soul with murderous thoughts.' It is said (Prov. xv. 18), 'A passionate man stirreth up strifes.' There are also the words of Jacob (Gen. xlix. 7), 'Cursed be their fury, because it was stubborn; and their wrath, because it was cruel.'

(4.) 2. *As to words.* We must guard against the growth of anger in word. Holy Scripture says (Prov. xii. 16), 'A fool immediately showeth his anger.' He does this in two ways; *a.* by revengeful upbraiding; and, *b.* by speaking proudly.

a. As to the one, our Lord says (St. Matt. v. 22), 'Whosoever shall say, Thou fool, shall be in danger of hell-fire.'

b. As to the other, He says, in the same place, 'Whosoever shall say to his brother, Raca, shall be in danger of the council.' Again, it is said (Prov. xv. 1), 'A mild answer breaketh wrath; but a harsh word stirreth up fury.'

(5.) 3. *As to deeds.* We must guard against the growth of anger in deeds. In all our works two things must be striven for carefully; *a.* to do justice, and, *b.* to love mercy. But anger hinders us in both. St. James says (i. 20), 'The anger of man worketh not the justice of God.' For even though he have the will, he has not the power. A certain wise man therefore said to one who had offended him, 'I would punish you if I were not angry.' As was said before, 'Anger hath no mercy, nor fury when it breaketh forth.' Again, it is said (Gen. xlix. 6), 'In their fury they slew a man.'

For these reasons our Lord teaches us not only to keep from murder, but even from anger. A good physician takes away the evil which is seen, but he takes away the root of the weakness as well, that it may not spring up again. Jesus therefore wills us to keep from the very beginnings of sin; and so from anger, which is the beginning of murder.

Prayer.

I.

O Jesus, Thou didst stand meekly before Pilate. Thou wast gentle to Thy fierce enemies. Thou didst forgive Thy murderers, and didst pray for them. Give me grace, dear Lord, so to restrain my anger that it may be a holy anger in Thee. Give me grace also to follow in Thy steps, and imitate Thee in Thy meekness, Thy patience, Thy forgiving spirit, and Thy long-suffering love.

Pluck out from my heart, Divine Master, the first beginnings of bitterness, and the seeds of all unkindness and evil will to others. Let long-suffering love like Thine, and a forgiving spirit like Thine, dwell always in my heart. Fill my soul with patience like Thy patience, and with the meekness of which Thou didst speak when Thou didst say to us, 'Learn of Me.' I pray with all my heart that the words of Thy Apostle may be fulfilled in me: 'Let this mind be in you which was also in Christ Jesus.' I hear Thy words, my Jesus : ' A new commandment I give to you, that ye love one another.' Keep bright in my soul the love of the brethren, that I may not pass from life to death. Help me, long-suffering Jesus !

II.

O Eternal Father, give me grace always to forgive my brother, as Thou dost forgive me. Let the light of the venerable prayer of Thy Son fill my soul, and teach me and guide me in the way of peace. O Heavenly Father, give me grace to live as Thy child.

III.

O Holy Ghost, my Sanctifier, I adore Thy patience and Thy forgiving love. As Thou art patient with me, so will I be patient with others ; and as Thou dost forgive me, so will I forgive others for Thy sake ; but I cannot do this without Thee. Help me, O most Blessed Spirit, whom I adore and praise and love.

IV.

O adorable Trinity, give me grace to put away from myself all wrong anger, all bitterness, all uncharitableness, all desire of revenge.   Thou art the Lord; vengeance is Thine; Thou wilt repay.   I kneel before Thy Throne, O adorable Trinity; and I give Thee all my heart and my soul.   O Blessed Trinity, O Blessed Trinity!

CHAPTER XI.

OF THE SIXTH COMMANDMENT OF THE LAW.

1. 'Thou shalt not commit adultery' (Ex. xx. 14).   After the forbiddal of murder there comes the forbiddal of adultery; and very fitting this is, for husband and wife are as one body.   God said (Gen. ii. 24), 'They shall be two in one flesh.'   After an injury, therefore, inflicted on a man himself, there can be none greater than an injury inflicted on a woman who is married to him.

N

Wife and husband alike are forbidden to commit adultery; but we will speak first of the adultery of the wife, for her sin has a look of being the greater. By adultery she commits three mortal sins: 1. unbelief; 2. treachery; 3. theft. These sins are indicated in Scripture, where it is said (Ecclus. xxiii. 32, 33), 'So every woman also that leaveth her husband and bringeth in an heir by another; for first she hath been unfaithful to the law of the Most High; and secondly she hath offended against her husband; and thirdly she hath fornicated in adultery, and hath had children of another man.'

1. **Unbelief.** She sins by unbelief; and that in three ways.

a. The law of God. She does not believe in the divine law, for it is God Himself who has forbidden adultery.

b. The ordinance of God. She goes against the ordinance of God. Our Lord said (St. Matt. xix. 4-6), 'Have ye not read that He who made man from the beginning made them male and female? And He said, For this cause shall a man leave father and mother and shall cleave to his wife, and they two shall be in one flesh. Therefore now they are not two, but one flesh. What therefore God hath joined together, let no man put asunder.'

c. The sacrament of God. She goes against the ordinances of the Church and against a sacrament of God. Marriage takes place in the face of the Church, and God is called upon as a witness, and as a surety that the husband and wife will keep their plighted faith. The prophet Malachias says (ii. 14), 'You have said, For what cause? Because the Lord hath been witness between thee, and the wife of thy youth, whom thou hast despised. Yet she was thy partner and the wife of thy covenant.' An adulterous woman therefore sins, *a.* against the law; *b.* against the ordinance; *c.* against the sacrament of God.

2. **Treachery.** She sins by treachery, be-

cause she forsakes her husband. St. Paul teaches this (1 Cor. vii. 4), ' The wife hath not power of her own body, but the husband.' Without the consent of her husband she cannot even observe chastity. In the sin of adultery, therefore, she is guilty of betrayal, in that she gives herself to another. So it is said (Prov. ii. 17, 18), ' She forsaketh the guide of her youth; and hath forgotten the covenant of her God.'*

3. **Theft.** She sins by theft. It must be so if she give to her husband the children of another. Indeed this is the greatest of thefts, when a whole inheritance is given to those who have no right to it.

In such a case she should strive to induce her children to adopt a state of poverty, or to take such steps at any rate as would hinder them from inheriting the property of her husband.

* Let husbands sinning in this way remember that these terrible words are true in substance also about themselves.

An adulterous woman therefore is, 1. sacrilegious ; 2. a traitoress ; 3. a thief.

II. **Sin of husbands.** The sin of husbands in this matter is no less grievous than the sin of the wife, though sometimes they flatter themselves that it is not. This is plain from three things.

1. **Equality.** We see it from the equality between the sins. St. Paul says (1 Cor. vii. 4), 'The husband also hath not power of his own body, but the wife.' So far then as regards duties of the married state, neither husband nor wife can do anything without the other's consent. It was to signify this that God did not make woman from the foot of man or from his head, but from one of his ribs. Marriage therefore is a perfect state only in the law of Christ. One Jew had many wives, but one wife had not many husbands ; and thus there was no equality.

2. **Strength.** We see it from the strength of the man. St. Peter says (1 Ep. iii. 7), ' Ye husbands, likewise dwelling with them

according to knowledge, giving honour to the woman as to the weaker vessel, and as to the coheirs of the grace of life, that your prayers be not hindered.' A man therefore breaks faith with his wife if he ask from her what he is not willing to give in return.

3. **Authority.** We see it from the aurity of the man. St. Paul says (1 Cor. xi. 3), 'The head of the woman is the man ;' and again (1 Cor. xiv. 34, 35), 'Let women keep silence in the churches ; for it is not permitted them to speak, but to be subject, as also the law saith. But if they would learn anything, let them ask their husbands at home. For it is a shame for a woman to speak in the church.' The man therefore is the teacher of the woman, and for this reason God gave the commandment at the beginning to Adam. Now as a priest is worse than a layman, and a bishop is worse than a priest, if they do not the things that they ought, because it is the duty of the priest and the bishop to teach others,

so an adulterous man, breaking faith with his wife, and not acting towards her as he ought to act, is worse than she would be, for he does not the things that he ought. Wives, however, should bear in mind our Lord's words about the Scribes and Pharisees (St. Matt. xxiii. 3), 'All things, therefore, whatsoever they shall say to you, observe and do; but according to their works do ye not: for they say and do not.'

III. 'Thou shalt not commit adultery.' As has been said, God has forbidden adultery both to husbands and wives.

We must also bear in mind that fornication is a mortal sin. The Apostle says (Heb. xiii. 4), 'Fornicators and adulterers God will judge;' and again (1 Cor. vi. 9, 10), 'Do not err, neither fornicators, nor idolaters, nor adulterers . . shall possess the kingdom of God.' Now, nothing but mortal sin keeps us out of the kingdom of God. Though in fornication there is not given the body of a wife, yet there is given the body of Christ; for our bodies are made

His, being consecrated to Him in Baptism. If, then, every one should refrain from injury to a wife, much more should he refrain from doing injury to Christ; as St. Paul says (1 Cor. vi. 15), 'Know you not that your bodies are the members of Christ? Shall I then take the members of Christ and make them members of a harlot? God forbid.' It would be heresy to deny that fornication is a deadly sin. Further, we see that this command forbids not only adultery, but every kind of fleshly sin. Again, it is heresy to say, as some have said, that the married state cannot be free from sin. For St. Paul says (Heb. xiii. 4), 'Marriage honourable in all, and the bed undefiled.' Husbands and wives may of course commit sin with regard to one another; but if they keep themselves in the grace of God, all their acts in the married state may be meritorious of eternal life. On the other hand these acts may be venial sins or they may be mortal sins. Husband and wife may desire children; and that is a virtuous desire. They may strive to fulfil every duty of their state; and then they act justly. On the other hand, they may indulge too much in sensual gratification; and so commit venial sin or mortal sin, as the case may be.

IV. Now these sins of uncleanness are forbidden for five reasons.

1. **Death of soul.** They destroy the soul. It is said (Prov. vi. 32), 'He that is an adulterer for the folly of his heart shall destroy his own soul.' He says, 'for the folly of his heart,' because in such a case the flesh rules the spirit.

2. **Death of body.** They deprive of life. It is said (Lev. xx. 10), 'If any man commit adultery with the wife of another, and defile his neighbour's wife, let them be put to death, both the adulterer and the adulteress;' and again (Deut. xxii. 21), 'They shall cast her out of the doors of her father's house, and the men of the city shall stone her to death, and she shall die.' Such a one may sometimes not be punished bodily;

but that is all the worse for the sinner. Bodily punishment, patiently borne, is a help towards forgiveness of sin. The punishment, nevertheless, will come in the next life.

3. **Waste of temporal gifts.** They waste goods which God gives us. So it is said of the Prodigal Son (St. Luke xv. 13), ' Not many days after, the younger son, gathering all together, went abroad into a far country, and there wasted his substance, living riotously.' Again (Ecclus. ix. 6), ' Give not thy soul to harlots in any point, lest thou destroy thyself and thy inheritance.'

4. **They cast a slur on the offspring.** It is said (Wisd. iii. 16, 17), ' The children of adulterers shall not come to perfection, and the seed of the unlawful bed shall be rooted out. If they live long they shall be nothing regarded, and their last old age shall be without honour.' Again (1 Cor. vii. 14), ' Otherwise your children should be unclean ; but now they are holy.'

5. **They deprive men, and still more**

women, of honour. It is said (Ecclus. ix. 10), 'Every woman that is a harlot, shall be trodden upon as dung in the way.' Of the man it is said (Prov. vi. 33), 'He gathereth to himself shame and dishonour, and his reproach shall not be blotted out.' St. Gregory also says that sins of the flesh, though of less guilt than sins of the spirit, are of greater infamy. **The reason** is because these things are in common with beasts; as it is said (Ps. xlviii. 13), 'Man, when he was in honour, did not understand; he is compared to senseless beasts, and is become like to them.'

Prayer.

I.

O Jesus, Thou God of the clean in heart, keep me from all defilements of the flesh. Save me from all stains on the white raiment in which I should walk with Thee. I am a member of Thy mystical body; and I have a great desire, dear Lord, to be always, body and soul, pure in Thy sight.

By Thy help I will never take Thy members and make them members of the devil. Save me, my own Brother, from vileness such as this.

Oftentimes, Jesus, Thou givest me Thy sweet body for food and Thy life-giving blood for drink. Then I carry Thee in my body. O, may I always glorify Thee, my God, according to Thy will.

Oftentimes in the adorable Sacrament of the Altar Thou givest me Thy soul. Thy soul, my Jesus, is the soul of God. It is made to the image and likeness of God. It is hypostatically united to God. It is Thy soul, Thou Eternal Word, Thou second Person of the ever-blessed Trinity, Thou begotten Wisdom of the Father. O, may I always glorify Thee, my God, when Thy soul dwelleth in me.

II.

O Holy Ghost, Thou God of light and healing, cleanse me with the sweetness of Thy fire. If Thou wilt help me I will never grieve Thee by faithlessness to Thy word. O my bright and beautiful God, keep me, soul and body, pure for Thyself. As I think of Thee, my heart leaps up to Thee with joy; Thy light enfolds me; Thy mercy heartens me; and Thy justice pierces me through and through. O adorable Spirit of God, I ask Thee in the gentleness of Thy love and the tenderness of Thy pity to give me a great loathing of all sins that come from the desire of the flesh. If I trust to Thee, and lean on Thee, I can overcome these temptations; but if I trust to myself I can only kill my soul.

O Thou all-holy God, watch over me, that I may inherit the blessing which Jesus promised to the clean in heart.

III.

Eternal Father, Thou hast given me Thy Son and Thy Spirit. With blessed Philip, the Apostle of Thy Son, I long to see Thee, the Father. I know that the sight of Thee is enough for every true desire. Nothing

that is defiled can come to Thee or enter
into Thy presence. O my heavenly Father,
keep me pure, and let my soul rest safely
in Thy everlasting arms.

***

CHAPTER XII.

OF THE SEVENTH COMMANDMENT OF THE LAW.

'THOU shalt not steal' (Ex. xx. 15).
God strictly forbade in His law all injury
of our neighbour. First, He forbade all
injury of our neighbour himself ; and
therefore He said, 'Thou shalt not kill.'
Next, He forbade all injury of the person
united to our neighbour, that is, his wife ;
and therefore He said, 'Thou shalt not
commit adultery.' Thirdly, He forbade all
injury done to our neighbour in his goods,
and therefore He said, 'Thou shalt not
steal.'

In the seventh commandment is forbidden the taking away of anything wrong-

fully.   Now a man may steal in five ways.

1. **Secretly.** He may take things secretly. Our Lord says (St. Matt. xxiv. 43), 'This know ye, that if the good man of the house knew at what hour the thief would come he would certainly watch, and would not suffer his house to be broken open.' Theft like this is to be condemned because it is a kind of treachery.

2. **Violently.** He may take things away with violence.   Theft like this is a greater injury than the first kind.   It is said (Job xxiv. 9, 10), 'They have violently robbed the fatherless, and stript the poor common people.   From the naked and them that go without clothing, and from the hungry they have taken away the ears of corn.'

Among such men as these are bad rulers and bad kings.   The prophet Sophonias says (iii. 3), 'Her princes are in the midst of her, like roaring lions; her judges are evening wolves; they left nothing for the morning.'   Acting thus they act against

God, whose will it is that they should reign justly; and who says (Prov. viii. 15), 'By Me kings reign and lawgivers decree just things.'

a. Theft. Sometimes they do these things after the manner of theft. Isaias says (i. 23), 'Thy princes are faithless, companions of thieves; they all love bribes and run after rewards. They judge not for the fatherless, and the widow's cause cometh not in to them.'

b. Force. Sometimes they act violently. The prophet Ezechiel says (xlvi. 18), 'The prince shall not take of the people's inheritance by violence, nor of their possession.'

c. Gain. Sometimes they make laws and statutes only for gain. Isaias says (x. 1, 2), 'Woe to them that make wicked laws, and when they write write injustice: to oppress the poor in judgment and do violence to the cause of the humble of My people, that widows might be their prey, and that they might rob the fatherless.'

St. Augustin says that every wicked dona-
tion is a theft ; and therefore he adds,
'What are such kingdoms as these but
dens of robbers ?'

3. **Defrauding workmen.** He may defraud workmen of their hire. It is said
(Lev. xix. 13), 'The wages of him that
hath been hired by thee shall not abide
with thee until the morning.'

This means, further, that every man must
give to others their due, whether it be to
the king, or the bishop, or the priest, and so
on. -St. Paul says (Rom. xiii. 7), 'Render,
therefore, to all men their dues : tribute
to whom tribute is due; custom to whom
custom; fear to whom fear; honour to
whom honour.' For we are bound to pay
our taxes to rulers who keep the peace.

4. **Cheating.** He may cheat in business.
It is said (Deut. xxv. 13), 'Thou shalt not
have diverse weights in thy bag, a greater
and a less :' and again (Lev. xix. 35, 36),
'Do not any unjust thing in judgment, in
rule, in weight, or in measure. Let the

o

balance be just and the weights equal, the bushel just and the sextary equal:' and again (Prov. xx. 23), 'Diverse weights are an abomination before the Lord; a deceitful balance is not good.' These things are said against the tradesmen who adulterate their wine with water, and so on.

Usury also is forbidden here. It is said in the Psalms (xiv. 1, 5), 'Lord, who shall dwell in Thy tabernacle? Or who shall rest on Thy holy hill?.... He that hath not put out his money to usury.' The commandment is also against money-changers, who act falsely in many ways, and against the sellers of clothes and other things.

Perhaps you will say, Why cannot I lend my money like my horse or my house? I answer that the sin is in selling a thing twice. Now, in a house there are two things, the house itself and the use of the house. It is one thing to have a house, and another to use it. I can sell the use without selling the house; and so in other

like things. Hence, if there be any commodities which consist in the use only,
and that use is in the parting with them,
I cannot deal with such possessions as I can
deal with a house. We use money in pay-
ing it away, and corn in eating it. If, therefore, we sell the use of these things, we sell
it twice over.*

* The laws about the lending of money have
changed because the way of using money has
changed; but the principle remains the same.
St. Thomas speaks according to the law of the
Church at his time, and that law could not have
been different from what it was, the use of money
being what it was.

Take the teaching on this subject in Gury's
Moral Theology (i. 853): ' Interest received for
the loan of a thing consumptible in the first use
is certainly unlawful. Such things are wine,
wheat, and the like. The reason for this is, that
the use of such commodities has no money value
independently of the thing which is borrowed;
while that thing only gives a title for the restitution of a like thing; nor is there any permanent
use which is equivalent to a price.'

Any one can see that this is the same doctrine
as the doctrine of St. Thomas. When therefore

5. **Buying dignities.** He may buy dignities, *a.* temporal, or, *b.* spiritual.

a. Temporal. Of these it is said (Job xx. 15), 'The riches which he hath swallowed he shall vomit up, and God shall draw them out of him.' For all tyrants who violently seize kingdoms or a province or a fief are robbers, and are bound to restitution.

b. Spiritual. Of these it is said by our Lord Himself (St. John x. 1), 'Amen, amen, I say unto you, he that entereth not by the door into the sheepfold, but climbeth up another way, the same is a thief and a

---

unbelievers say that the Church has contradicted herself in this matter, we answer that she has done nothing of the sort. The change is in the use of money, and not in the Church's teaching. As to things which change, the Church is guided by the Holy Ghost to make laws suited to the times. Money now is not a commodity consumptible in the first use as it was in the days of St. Thomas; but a commodity which can be itself bought and sold and used. Its use therefore now has a money value.

robber.' They, therefore, who are guilty of simony are robbers.

II. 'Thou shalt not steal.' This commandment, as has been said, forbids all wrong taking away from others; and there are four reasons why we should strive carefully to keep it.

1. **The grievousness of the sin.** It is in Ecclesiasticus likened to murder (xxxiv. 25), 'The bread of the needy is the life of the poor ; he that defraudeth them thereof is a man of blood.' Then it is added (vv. 26, 27), 'He that taketh away the bread gotten by sweat is like him that killeth his neighbour. He that sheddeth blood and he that defraudeth the labourer of his hire are brothers.'

2. **The nature of the danger.** There is no sin so dangerous as this. Sins, as we know, cannot be forgiven without satisfaction and repentance. Now it is easy to repent of other sins. Thus, a man, when his anger cools, is sorry for killing any one; and when temptations of the flesh pass away,

he is sorry for sins of uncleanness. So it is with many other sins. But as to the sin of theft, though a man repent of it, yet he cannot easily make restitution, especially as he is bound not only to make restitution for what he has taken, but also for the loss that he has caused the person from whom he stole. Besides, he is also bound to do penance for his sin. Hence the prophet Habacuc says (ii. 6), 'Woe to him that heapeth together that which is not his own ; how long doth he load himself with thick clay ?" He calls the stolen things thick clay, because a man does not easily get free from them.

3. **The uselessness of the things taken.** They are not useful, either, *a.* spiritually, or, *b.* temporally.

a. Spiritually. Spiritually they are useless, as it is said (Prov. x. 2), 'Treasures of wickedness shall profit nothing.' Riches may be made spiritually useful for alms and sacrifices. In this sense it is said (Prov. xiii. 8), 'The ransom of a man's life is his riches.' Of riches, however, that are not our own, Isaias says (lxi. 8), 'I am the Lord that love judgment, and hate robbery in a holocaust.' In Ecclesiasticus also (xxxiv. 24), it is said, 'He that offereth sacrifice of the goods of the poor is as one that sacrificeth the son in the presence of his father.'

b. Temporally. Temporally they are useless, for they soon waste away. Habacuc says (ii. 9-11), 'Woe to him that gathereth together an evil covetousness to his house, that his nest may be on high, and thinketh he may be delivered out of the hand of evil. Thou hast devised confusion to thy house; thou hast cut off many people, and thy soul hath sinned. For the stone shall cry out of the wall, and the timber that is between the joints of the building shall answer.', Again (Prov. xxviii. 8), 'He that heapeth together riches by usury and loan gathereth them for him that will be bountiful to the poor.' Again (Prov. xiii. 22), 'The substance of the sinner is kept for the just.'

4. The singular injury which they cause. They make other things waste away. Nay, they are like fire kindled among the straw. Job says (xv. 34), 'Fire shall devour their tabernacles who love to take bribes.' Think also of the injury such a one does, not only to his own soul, but also to the souls of his children, who are bound* to restitution.

Prayer.

O Jesus, Thou just Judge, Thou Lawgiver who always doest right, give me grace to be just in all my dealings with others. Let me never overreach my brother, or cheat him, or defraud him in business. Thou hatest false measures and unequal weights and lying words. O dear Jesus, save me from being a cheat; save me from being a thief; save me from being a liar for the sake of defrauding others.

* The Saint is speaking of possessors 'malæ fidei;' that is, of those who know of the theft, and derive benefit from it.

Do Thou, dear Lord, fill my soul with a great love of justice. May I always do to others as I desire that they may do to me, and may I never do to others what I would not like them to do to me! Let uprightness and truthfulness and fair dealing and a spirit of justice reign in my heart. Save me from meanness and trickery and craftiness and baseness of soul.

Thou art a King of equity, O Jesus, and a Judge of justice. Thy people live peacefully in Thy kingdom, and none make them afraid.

As I know, Divine Master, that it is my duty to pay my debts, give me grace not to delay, but always promptly to do what is right. Let me not steal credit or reputation from another, nor ever keep back from others that which is their due.

O Thou Judge, who dost decree righteous judgment, give me a spirit of justice, which faileth not nor wavereth.

CHAPTER XIII.

THE EIGHTH COMMANDMENT OF THE LAW.

'Thou shalt not bear false witness against thy neighbour' (Ex. xx. 16). God, having forbidden us to injure our neighbour in deeds, now goes on to forbid us injuring him in words; and therefore He says, 'Thou shalt not bear false witness.' Now we may bear false witness in two ways, that is, (1.) in judgment, and (2.) in our common talk.

I. (1.) **In judgment.** We may do this in three ways, as there are three persons who can sin against this command.

1. *There is the false accuser.* Of him it is said (Lev. xix. 16), 'Thou shalt not be a detractor or a whisperer among the people. Thou shalt not stand against the blood of thy neighbour.'

But mark: as you must not say what is false, so you must not conceal what is true. Our Lord says (St. Matt. xviii. 15), 'If thy brother shall offend against thee, go and rebuke him.'

2. *There is the lying witness.* It is said (Prov. xix. 9), ' A false witness shall not be unpunished.' This command includes those that have gone before, for sometimes such a witness is a murderer, and sometimes a thief, and so on. Such are to be severely punished, as it is said (Deut. xix. 18-21), ' When, after most diligent search, they shall find that the false witness hath told a lie against his brother, they shall render to him as he meant to do to his brother, and thou shalt take away the evil out of the midst of thee, that others hearing may fear and may not dare to do such things. Thou shalt not pity him, but shalt require life for life, eye ·for eye, tooth for tooth, hand for hand, foot for foot.' Again (Prov. xxv. 18), ' A man that beareth false witness against his neighbour is like a dart, and a sword, and a sharp arrow.'

3. *There is the unjust judge.* It is said (Lev. xix. 15), ' Thou shalt not do that which is unjust, nor judge unjustly. Respect not the person of the poor, nor honour

the countenance of the mighty, but judge thy neighbour according to justice.'

(2.) **In common talk.** As to this there are five ways in which men sin.

1. *There are detractors.*   Of these St. Paul says (Rom. i. 30), 'Detractors, hateful to God.'   He says hateful to God, because nothing is so dear to a man as his good name; as it is said (Eccles. vii. 2), 'A good name is better than precious ointments;' and again (Prov. xxii. 1), 'A good name is better than great riches, and good favour is above silver and gold.'   But detractors take away this good favour and good name; as it is said (Eccles. x. 11), 'If a serpent bite in silence, he that back-biteth secretly is nothing better.'   Hence detractors, if they would be saved, must undo the evil that they have done.   Again (Wisd. i. 11), 'Refrain your tongue from detraction.'

2. *There are, they who listen to detraction willingly and gladly.* Of these it is said (Ecclus. xxviii. 28), 'Hedge in thy ears

with thorns; hear not a wicked tongue; and make doors and bars to thy mouth.'

No one ought to listen to a detractor with pleasure. On the contrary, the listener should look at him with a stern and disapproving face. It is said (Prov. xxv. 23), ' The north wind driveth away rain; so doth a sad countenance a backbiting tongue.'

3. *There are whisperers.* They tell over and over again everything that they hear. Of these it is said (Prov. vi. 16, 19), ' Six things there are which the Lord hateth, and the seventh His soul detesteth : . . . . him that soweth discord among brethren.' Again (Ecclus. xxviii. 15), ' The whisperer and the double-tongued is accursed; for he hath troubled many that were at peace.' Again (vv. 20-24), ' He that hearkeneth to it shall never have rest, neither shall he have a friend in whom he may repose. The stroke of a whip maketh a blue mark, but the stroke of the tongue will break the bones. Many have fallen by the edge of the sword, but not so many as have perished

by their own tongue. Blessed is he that is defended from a wicked tongue ; that hath not drawn the yoke thereof, and that hath not been bound in its bands: for its yoke is a yoke of iron, and its bands are bands of brass.'

4. *There are flatterers.* It is said (Ps. ix. 24, or x. 3, acc. to Hebrews), ' The sinner is praised in the desires of his soul, and the unjust man is blessed.' Isaias also says (iii. 12), ' O My people, they that call thee blessed, the same deceive thee, and destroy the way of thy steps.' Again (Ps. cxl. 5), ' The just man shall correct me in mercy and shall reprove me ; but let not the oil of the sinner fatten my head.'

5. *There are murmurers.* This sin is chiefly found in those who are under authority. St. Paul says (1 Cor. x. 10), ' Neither do you murmur, as some of them murmured, and were destroyed by the destroyer.' So it is said (Wisd. i. 11), 'Keep yourselves therefore from murmuring, which profiteth nothing.' Again (Prov. xxv. 15),

'By patience a prince shall be appeased; and a soft tongue shall break hardness.'

II. 'Thou shalt not bear false witness.' In this commandment is forbidden every lie. It is said (Ecclus. vii. 13, 14), 'Devise not a lie against thy brother, neither do the like against thy friend. Be not willing to make any manner of lie, for the custom thereof is not good.' There are four reasons for this:

1. **Likeness to the devil.** Such a one is made a child of the devil. We know by a man's speech from what country he comes. So we read (St. Matt. xxvi. 73), 'After a little while they came that stood by, and said to Peter, Surely thou art one of them, for even thy speech doth discover thee.' Our Lord said (St. John viii. 44), 'You are of your father, the devil; and the desires of your father you will do. . . . When he speaketh a lie, he speaketh of his own; for he is a liar, and the father thereof.'

a. Certain men, therefore, are of the race of the devil, and are called children of the devil, because they are liars. The devil lied in the beginning to Eve (Gen. iii. 4) : ' No, you shall not die the death ; for God doth know that in what day soever you shall eat thereof, your eyes shall be opened, and you shall be as gods, knowing good and evil.

b. Other men, however, are called the sons of God because they speak the truth ; for God is truth. Our Lord prayed thus (St. John xvii. 17), ' Sanctify them in truth. Thy word is truth.'

2. **The breaking up of civil society.** Men now dwell together ; but this would not be possible if they did not speak the truth. St. Paul says (Eph. iv. 25), ' Putting away lying, speak ye the truth, every man with his neighbour ; for we are members one of another.' So Zacharias (viii. 16, 17), ' These then are the things which you shall do : Speak ye truth every one to his neighbour ; judge ye truth and judgment of peace in your gates. And let none of you imagine evil in your hearts against

his friend; and love not a false oath; for all these are the things that I hate, saith the Lord.'

3. **The loss of our good name.** No one believes a liar even when he happens to be speaking the truth. It is said (Ecclus. xxxiv. 4), 'What can be made clean by the unclean? and what truth can come from that which is false?'

4. **The loss of our souls.** A liar destroys his own soul, as the Scripture says (Wisd. i. 11), 'The mouth that lieth killeth the soul.'* Again (Ps. v. 7), 'Thou wilt destroy all that speak a lie.' Hence it is clear that there are lies which are mortal sins.

III. We see, therefore, that some lies are venial, and some are mortal.

1. **About the faith.** It is a mortal sin to lie about those truths that have to do with the faith. This pertains to bishops, teachers, and preachers, and is the worst kind of lie. St. Peter says (2 Ep. ii. 1),

* Vulg. Os quod mentitur occidit animam.

P

'There were also false prophets among the
people, even as there shall be among you
lying teachers, who shall bring in sects of
perdition, and deny the Lord who bought
them, bringing upon themselves swift destruction.'

2. **Love of deceiving.** Some speak on
these matters in order that they may seem to
know ; as Isaias says (lvii. 4), 'Upon whom
have you jested ? Upon whom have you
opened your mouth wide and put out your
tongue ? Are you not wicked children, a
lying seed ?'*

3. **Against our neighbour.** Some tell
lies to do harm to their neighbour. St.
Paul says (Col. iii. 9), 'Lie not one to
another.' These last two kinds of lying
are also mortal sins.

Again, some tell lies, 1. for themselves,
and, 2. for others.

1. **For themselves:** and that in many
ways.

a. *False humility.* Some tell lies out of

.* Vulg. Semen mendax.

a false humility even in confession. Of them St. Augustin says, ' As a man should take care not to conceal what he has done, so he should take care not to say what he has not done.' Job says (xiii. 7), ' Hath God any need of your lie, that you should speak deceitfully for Him ?' Again (Ecclus. xix. 23, 24), ' There is one that humbleth himself wickedly, and his inward parts are full of deceit ; and there is one that submitteth himself exceedingly with a great lowliness.'

b. False shame. Some tell lies from a false shame. Thus a man says a thing, believing it to be true : suddenly remembers it is false, and is ashamed to correct himself. Of this it is said (Ecclus. iv. 30), ' In no wise speak against the truth ; but be ashamed of the lie of thy ignorance.'*

c. Our advantage. Some tell lies for

---

* This refers to culpable ignorance. St. Thomas here evidently is thinking of a case where there are reasons why a man should correct his statement.

their own gain. They wish (*a.*) to get some good for themselves, or (*b.*) to avoid some evil. Of these Isaias says (xxviii. 15), 'We have placed our hope in lies, and by falsehood we are protected;' and again it is said (Prov. x. 4), 'He that trusteth to lies feedeth the winds.'

2. **For others.** Some tell lies for the sake of another. They endeavour thus to save some one, *a.* from death, or, *b.* from danger, or, *c.* even from any loss. This must not be done. It is said (Ecclus. iv. 26), 'Accept no person against thy own person, nor against thy soul a lie.'

In joke. Some tell lies in joke. Even this should not be done, because of getting into a habit which may lead us to sin mortally by lying. It is said in Wisdom (iv. 12), 'The bewitching of vanity obscureth good things.'*

* It would be well if we all hated venial sin more than we do; for though it is not an offence against God in the same sense as mortal sin, yet it makes God angry with us. Then we would

Prayer.

O Holy Ghost, save me from all wrong doubt about my neighbour, from all rash suspicion, and from all rash judgment.

Give me, O Holy Spirit, a hatred of lying, and give me also strength always to speak the truth. I desire to speak truthfully in great things and in little things, that my words may be pleasing to Thee.

Make me watchful, Blessed Spirit, over my thoughts and my tongue, that I may not injure my neighbours by detraction or by calumny or by any kind of backbiting. Let me remember always that they are Thy temples, members of the mystical

---

always be on our guard with great care against telling even the smallest lies. Lies may become mortal sins from the circumstances, as St. Thomas points out here. Sometimes that may happen easily. We should also lay to heart what he says about a habit of telling any lies leading us on to tell greater lies. In this way, step by step, we may go on till we quench the Spirit of God in our souls.

Body of Jesus, and fellow-heirs of everlasting life.

If ever, through my weakness, I should injure my neighbour in this way, give me grace, O loving Spirit, to make restitution at any cost, and to keep Thy law of justice.

* * *

CHAPTER XIV.

OF THE NINTH COMMANDMENT OF THE LAW.*

'THOU shalt not covet thy neighbour's house .... nor anything that is his' (Ex. xx. 17). The great difference between the law of God and the law of man is that, whereas man's law only judges deeds and words, God's law judges these and the thoughts also. This could not be other-

---

* St. Thomas follows the order in Ex. xx. 17. 'Thou shalt not covet thy neighbour's house ; neither shalt thou desire his wife ;' and not the order in Deut. x. 21, 'Thou shalt not covet thy neighbour's wife nor his house.' The Catechism follows the order in Deuteronomy.

wise; for man's law comes by men, and they only judge that which is outwardly seen; but the divine law comes from God, who sees all things, both outward and inward. So God said to Samuel (1 Kings xvi. 7), 'I do not judge according to the look of man; for man seeth those things that appear, but the Lord beholdeth the heart.' David also says (Ps. lxxii. 26), 'Thou art the God of my heart.'

The commandments about words and deeds having been spoken of, it remains to speak of those which regard our thoughts. With God the will is taken for the deed; and therefore He says, 'Thou shalt not covet.' Not only are we forbidden to take anything unlawfully from our neighbour, but we are forbidden even to desire to have that which is his. There are six reasons for this.

1. **Our weakness.** There is our weakness because of concupiscence; and concupiscence may be said to be in a way infinite. Now every wise man ought to seek some

definite end before him; nay more, no one ought to walk on a way that is without an end. The Scripture says (Eccles. v. 9), 'A covetous man shall not be satisfied with money; and he that loveth riches shall reap no fruit from them.' So Isaias (v. 8), 'Woe to you that join house to house and lay field to field, even to the end of the place.'

The reason why this kind of desire never can be satisfied is because man's heart was made for the possession of God. Hence, as we saw in the second chapter, St. Augustin says, 'Thou hast made us, O Lord, for Thyself, and our hearts are restless till they rest in Thee.' Therefore anything less than God cannot fill the heart of man. Of God it is said (Ps. cii. 5), 'He satisfieth thy desire with good things.'

2. **Disquiet of soul.** Covetousness destroys peace of soul; and this peace is a thing greatly to be desired. The covetous are always anxious about gaining what they have not, and about keeping safely what

they have. It is said (Eccles. v. 11), 'The fulness of the rich will not suffer him to sleep.' Our Lord says (St. Matt. vi. 21), 'Where thy treasure is, there is thy heart also.' For this reason, as St. Gregory points out, our Lord likened riches to thorns (St. Luke viii. 14): 'That which fell among thorns are they who have heard, and going their way are choked with the cares and riches and pleasures of this life, and yield no fruit.'

3. **Hoarding.** It makes riches useless. The riches of the covetous are useless, both for themselves and others. All that they do with them is to hoard them up. So it is said (Ecclus xiv. 3), 'Riches are not comely for a covetous man and a niggard; and what should an envious man do with gold?'

4. **Injustice.** It takes away the equity of justice. We read (Ex. xxiii. 8), 'Thou shalt not take bribes which blind even the wise and pervert the words of the just.' And again (Ecclus. xxxi. 5), 'He that lov-

eth gold shall not be justified, and he that
followeth after corruption shall be filled
with it.'

5. **Mortal sin.** It kills the love of God
and our neighbour. St. Augustin teaches
that the more a man has of charity the less
covetous he is, and the more covetous he is
the less charity he has. It is said (Ecclus.
vii. 20), 'Do not transgress against thy
friend concerning money, nor despise thy
dearest brother for the sake of gold.' Thus
it destroys the love of our neighbour, and
it also destroys the love of God. Our Lord
says (St. Matt. vi. 24), 'No man can serve
two masters : . . . . you cannot serve God
and mammon.'

6. **All iniquity.** It leads to every kind
of wickedness. According to the Apostle
covetousness is the root of all evil. For
if it be rooted in the heart, a man for the
sake of gain will commit murder and theft,
and all kinds of sin. The Apostle therefore says (1 Tim. vi. 9, 10), 'They that will
become rich fall into temptation, and into

the snare of the devil, and into many un-profitable and hurtful desires, which drown men in destruction and perdition. For the desire of money is the root of all evils; which some coveting have erred from the faith and have entangled themselves in many sorrows.'

Observe that covetousness is a mortal sin when the goods of our neighbour are desired without reason; but a venial sin when they are desired with reason.*

Prayer.

O adorable Trinity, give me a spirit of justice and of brotherly love. Let me al-ways be content with what Thou givest to me, and let me not sin against Thee by coveting my neighbour's goods. If I have

---

* This statement is much the same as that in the Catechism, about 'all ... unjust desires of our neighbours' goods and profits.' Sins of covet-ousness without an excusing reason are mortal, and sins of covetousness with an excusing reason are venial. But in both cases the matter also must be considered.

Thee, my God, I have all things, and all other things are nothing without Thee.

O my Maker and my Reward, Thou knowest what is best for me, and I give myself, all that I am and all that I have, utterly in love and confidence to Thee. I believe in Thee, and love Thee, and trust Thee with all my heart and soul and strength.

All the beasts of the forest, O my God, are Thine ; the cattle on the hills and the oxen. Thou dost give me that which is best in Thine eyes. I am content with what Thou givest, and what Thou givest not I desire not.

I thank Thee, O bountiful God, for all that Thou givest to others ; and I bless Thee for Thy love and beneficence and watchful care. Thy graciousness and Thy generosity are infinite, as Thou art. In Thee and by Thee Thy creatures live. Thou art my God and my all. O ever-blessed Trinity, I desire nothing but Thee.

CHAPTER XV.

THE TENTH COMMANDMENT OF THE LAW.

'Thou shalt not desire his wife' (Ex. xx. 17). Blessed John says (1 Ep. ii. 16), 'All that is in the world is the desire of the flesh, and the desire of the eyes, and the pride of life, which is not of the Father but is of the world.' In these three things then are to be found all that we can desire.* Now two of these, namely, the desire of the eyes and the pride of life, are forbidden in the commandment, 'Thou shalt not covet thy neighbour's house.' For in the word 'house' is understood that height by which avarice is indicated, as in the Psalms (cxi. 3), 'Glory and wealth shall be in his house.' A man, therefore, who covets the house of his neighbour covets his honours and riches. So after this command there is given another by which the desire of the flesh is forbidden. God said, 'Neither shalt thou covet his wife.'

* That is, desire in a wrong way.

I. You must bear in mind that after the Fall, because of the corruption of sin, no one escaped concupiscence except Christ and the glorious Virgin. Moreover, when concupiscence is present, it is present either with venial sin or mortal sin when it reigns in us.* The Apostle says (Rom. vi. 12),

* As the Saint explains, a few lines further on: when it reigns in us 'so as to fulfil the lusts thereof.'

Gury (i. 15) gives the following definition of concupiscence: Concupiscence, by which the act is defined, is 'a movement of the sensitive appetite springing from the imagination of good or evil' (*St. Thom.* in l. 3, sent. dist. 26, q. 1, a. 1), and it draws us, especially in a more intense way, to some apprehended good, or turns us from some apprehended evil.

It is also called an affection or even a passion, because along with its acts there 'is excited some material passion in the body.'

Cf. *Suarez in* 1 *S. Thom. de Anima,* l. 5, c. 5, n. 1 ; and in 1, 2, *S. Thom. de Passionibus,* Disp. I., sect. 3.

'This holy Synod confesses and believes that concupiscence or fuel of sin (*fomes*) remains in the baptised. Being left for the conflict, it has no power to injure those who do not consent to

'Let not sin reign in your mortal body.'
He does not say, 'Let it not be;' for he
himself had written (Rom. vii. 18), 'I
know that there dwelleth not in me, that
is to say, in my flesh, that which is good.'
Now sin reigns in our flesh in three ways,
when concupiscence reigns in us by our
consenting.

1. **The heart.** We give consent in our
hearts. St. Paul, therefore, adds to his
words, 'Let not sin reign in your mortal
bodies,' these other words (Rom. vi. 12),

---

it, but resist it manfully by the grace of Jesus
Christ. Nay more, he who striveth lawfully is
crowned. This Holy Synod declares that concupiscence, which the Apostle sometimes calls sin,
has never been understood by the Catholic Church
to be called sin because it is truly and properly
sin in the baptised, but because it comes from
sin and leads to sin.'

Council of Trent, Sess. V., *decr. de peccato
orig. 5.*

'Labour as a good soldier of Jesus Christ. . . .
He also that striveth for the mastery is not
crowned unless he strive lawfully' (2 *Tim.* ii.
3, 5).

about thee in the ways of the city, nor
.wander up and down in the streets thereof.
Turn away thy face-from a woman dressed
up, and gaze not about upon another's
beauty. For many have perished by the ,
beauty of a woman; and hereby lust is en-
kindled as a fire.... Many by admiring
the beauty of another man's wife have become reprobate.'* Again (Prov. vi. 27),
'Can a man hide fire in his bosom, and his
garments not burn?' Remember the warning given by the angels to Lot. He had
not to stay anywhere in the country near
Sodom (Gen. xix. 17): 'They brought him
forth and set him without the city, and

---

* With regard to sins like these which destroy
so many thousands of souls, there is one thing
which we must bear in mind. These words of
the Holy Ghost are spoken, in the first instance, ,
to men; but of course, in substance, they are
also spoken to women. ⁄ In like manner, therefore, women must apply His warnings to themselves. Blessed is the soul that listens to all the
words of the Holy Ghost. 'Thou shalt not covet
thy neighbour's wife' implies this: 'Thou shalt
not covet thy neighbour's husband.'

there they spoke to him, saying, Save thy life, look not back, neither stay thou in all the country about; but save thyself in the mountain, lest thou also be consumed.'

2. **A guard against bad thoughts.** We must not allow such thoughts to find an entrance into our minds at all; if we do, they will excite us to all kinds of bad desires. Our safety as to wrong thoughts is to be found in mortification and penance. As St. Paul says (1 Cor. ix. 27), 'I chastise my body and bring it into subjection; lest, perhaps, when I have preached to others I myself should become a castaway.'

3. **Prayer.** We must persevere in prayer. The Psalmist says (cxxvi. 1), 'Unless the Lord build the house, they labour in vain that build it.' It is also said (Wisd. viii. 21), 'As I knew that I could not otherwise be continent unless God gave it, and this also was a point of wisdom to know whose gift it was, I went to the Lord and besought Him. . . . with my whole heart.' Our Lord Himself said (St. Matt. xvii. 20),

'This kind is not cast out but by prayer and fasting.'

You will easily see that this must be so. If two men be fighting and you wish to be of use to one and not to the other, you must give help to one and not give it to the other. Now there is a ceaseless warfare going on between the flesh and the spirit. If, then, you wish to succour the spirit, you must give it what help you can by prayer, for by prayer you can give it great help. If, on the other hand, you wish to withdraw succour from the flesh, you can do this by fasting; for it is by fasting that the flesh is weakened.

4. **Industry.** We must be industrious at our work. As we saw before (ch. viii. II. (1.) 3.), Scripture says (Ecclus. xxxiii. 29), 'Idleness hath taught much evil.' In Ezechiel also it is said (xvi. 49), 'This was the iniquity of Sodom thy sister—pride, fulness of bread, abundance, and the idleness of her and of her daughters.' St. Jerome also, quoted before in the same

place, says, 'Always be busy about something good, that the devil may find you occupied.' Now among all occupations the best is the study of the Holy Scriptures. Hence St. Jerome says to Paulinus, 'Love the study of Scripture, and you will not love the sins of the flesh.'

You see, then, that there are two principal roots of all the commandments, that is to say, (1.) the love of God and (2.) the love of our neighbour.

(1.) **The love of God.** He who loves God must of necessity do three things.

1. **He must have no other God.** For this reason it is said, 'Thou shalt not have strange gods before Me.'

2. **He must honour God.** For this reason it is said, 'Thou shalt not take the name of the Lord thy God in vain.'

3. **He must freely find his rest in God.** For this reason it is said, 'Remember that thou keep holy the Sabbath-day.'

(2.) **The love of our neighbour.** He who loves his neighbour must do two things.

1. He must show him due honour. For this reason it is said, 'Honour thy father and thy mother.'

2. He must keep from doing him any harm. This he must do in three ways :

a. In deed.

> (*a.*) *As to himself.* For this reason it is said, 'Thou shalt not kill.'
>
> (*b.*) *As to his wife.* For this reason it is said, 'Thou shalt not commit adultery.'
>
> (*c.*) *As to his goods.* For this reason it is said, 'Thou shalt not steal.'

b. In word. For this reason it is said, 'Thou shalt not bear false witness against thy neighbour.'

c. In thought.

> (*a.*) 'Thou shalt not covet thy neighbour's goods.'
>
> (*b.*) 'Thou shalt not covet thy neighbour's wife.'

This, then, is what has been taught

about those ten words of which Jesus said (St. Matt. xix. 17), 'If thou wilt enter into life, keep the commandments.'

Prayer.

O Eternal Father, I am Thy child; let me not sin against Thee by any wrong thoughts or wrong desires. Let me not sin against my neighbours in that which is nearest and dearest to them. Give me victory in every temptation, by Thy Holy Spirit, for the sake of Thy Son, Jesus.

O Jesus, help me and save me. O Holy Ghost, help me and save me. I desire to keep myself from every shadow of impurity, and from the faintest beginnings of sin. O Jesus, Thou didst die for me.

O Holy Ghost, Thou art my Sanctifier. Help me, who am very weak, O Blessed Spirit of love, to keep all the commandments of God.

O adorable Trinity, help and bless me, whom Thou hast made in Thy own image and likeness. Save me, whom Thou didst create for Thyself. O Blessed Trinity, O Blessed Trinity, O Blessed Trinity.

Thanksgiving for the Ten Commandments.

I listen to Thee, my God, amid the thunders of Horeb, and I watch for Thee amid the lightnings of Sinai. Thy voice is terrible and sweet. Thy brightness is like a devouring fire. Thy light is sweet as Thy love, and Thy love is gleaming as the splendour of Thy light.

O my Maker, my Redeemer, my Sanctifier, I bless Thee for all Thy gifts; but now I bless Thee for Thy commandments. Thy commandment is exceedingly broad. Thou dost teach me Thy law, and I delight in it; for I believe in it and love it and walk in it day by day. Thy statutes are truth and Thy ways are truth. Thou art near, O Lord, to those who seek Thee. Thy commandments are my meditation and my food in the house of my pilgrimage. They have a beauty that comes from Thee, and they are the blessedness of the soul that has joy in them. By them Thou givest me wisdom. All Thy commandments are faithful; they are confirmed for ever and ever; they are made in truth and justice. My lips shall utter a hymn to Thee, the living God; for Thou dost teach me Thy law.

O my God, Thou didst come down on Mount Sinai in fire, and the smoke rose from it as from a furnace, and all the mount was terrible.

Thou didst speak Thy ten words from the midst of the fire and the cloud and the darkness, and Thou didst write them in two tables of stone. I bless and praise Thee for these life-giving words; and I pray that I may always have them in my heart.

O Father, Son, and Holy Ghost, adorable Trinity, give me grace to keep Thy commandments that I may enter into life, and see Thee, face to face and eye to eye, who art blessed for evermore.

Works of the Rev. Father Rawes, D.D.

THE LIBRARY OF THE HOLY GHOST.

Vol. I.

THE BREAD OF LIFE: St. Thomas Aquinas on the Adorable Sacrament of the Altar. With Prayers and Thanksgivings added for Holy Communion. With a Letter by the Cardinal Archbishop of WESTMINSTER.

Vol. II., *Ready for press.*

THE GIFT OF GOD; or St. Thomas Aquinas on the Holy Ghost. With a Way of Hearing Mass in Honour of the Holy Ghost; Prayers of Saints, and other Prayers; Hymns; and the Little Handbook of the Archconfraternity.

*** This will be the Handbook of the Archconfraternity. The Little Handbook (No. 2 in the Series of Little Books of the Holy Ghost) will always be printed as now.

In preparation,

Vol. III.

SUAREZ ON THE MOTHER OF GOD.

Vol. IV.

ST. BONAVENTURE ON THE SEVEN GIFTS OF THE HOLY GHOST.

Vol. V.

ST. BASIL ON THE HOLY GHOST.

Works of the Rev. Father Rawes, D.D.

LITTLE BOOKS OF THE HOLY GHOST.

No. I.

ST. THOMAS AQUINAS ON THE COM-
MANDMENTS. With a Letter by the Cardinal
Archbishop of WESTMINSTER.

No. II.

THE LITTLE HANDBOOK OF THE ARCH-
CONFRATERNITY. Fourth Edition.

No. III., *In the press.*

ST. THOMAS AQUINAS ON THE LORD'S
PRAYER.

No. IV., *In preparation.*

THE HOLY GHOST, THE SANCTIFIER. By
the Cardinal Archbishop of WESTMINSTER.

No. V.

ST. THOMAS AQUINAS ON THE APOSTLES'
CREED.

No. VI.

OUR LADY THE HANDMAID OF THE
HOLY GHOST. By One of His Servants.

No. VII.

CARDINAL BELLARMINE'S ASCENT OF
THE MIND TO GOD.

Works of the Rev. Father Rawes, D.D.

DEVOTIONS FOR THE WAY OF THE CROSS. With Drawings by N. H. J. WESTLAKE. Boards, 2s. 6d.; cloth neat, 4s. 6d.

HOMEWARD. Second Edition, 3s. 6d.

GOD IN HIS WORKS. A Course of Five Sermons. Cloth, 2s. 6d..

THE BELOVED DISCIPLE, or St. John the Evangelist. In 1 vol., neat cloth, 3s. 6d. Second Edition, with a Sermon on St. John by St. Charles Borromeo.

GREAT TRUTHS IN LITTLE WORDS. Third Edition, neat cloth, 3s. 6d.

°**THE EUCHARISTIC MONTH.** From the Latin of Father LERCARI, S.J. Third Edition, 6d.; cloth, 1s.

⁶**TWELVE VISITS TO OUR LADY AND THE HEAVENLY CITY OF GOD.** Third Edition, 8d.

SEPTEM: SEVEN WAYS OF HEARING MASS. Tenth Edition, 2s.; bound, red edges, 2s. 6d.; calf, 4s.

°**DEVOTIONS FOR THE SOULS IN PURGATORY.** Fourth Edition, cloth, 2s.; to which are added, A Way of Hearing Mass for the Dead, and The Doctrine of Suarez on Purgatory.

°**NINE VISITS TO THE BLESSED SACRAMENT.** From the Canticle of Canticles. Third Edition, 6d.

* Or in 1 vol., VISITS AND DEVOTIONS, neat cloth, 3s.